rororo

ro
ro
ro

rororo sprachen
Herausgegeben von Ludwig Moos

Jobstart, Beförderung oder Verabschiedung, Abteilungsfeier, Betriebsversammlung oder Mitarbeitermeeting, Einweihung, Jubiläum oder Jahresrückblick, Zukauf, Fusion oder feindliche Übernahme, Messe, Verkaufsveranstaltung oder Aktionärsversammlung – das Geschäftsleben ist voller Anlässe, bei denen die Rede stimmen muß. *Spice up Your Speeches* liefert eine Fülle von Beispielen, zeigt, was schiefgehen kann, und hilft mit einem Kompaktkurs Rhetorik, jede Herausforderung zu meistern. Die Toncassette zum Buch (60844) schärft das Ohr für die Feinheiten.

Dr. René Bosewitz ist Native Speaker und bereitet in einer deutschen Zweigstelle der London Chamber of Commerce Firmenangehörige auf einschlägige sprachliche Prüfungen vor. Er trainiert zudem seit vielen Jahren Manager aus Banken und Industrie in Business English. Bei rororo sprachen hat er *Better Your English* (60802) und zusammen mit Robert Kleinschroth *Joke Your Way Through English Grammar* (8527) und *Joke by Joke to Conversation* (8795) veröffentlicht.

Robert Kleinschroth unterrichtet Englisch am Gymnasium und an der Universität Heidelberg. Er hat zwanzig Jahre Praxis in der Erwachsenenbildung und leitete fünfzehn Jahre lang die Sprachabteilung eines Großunternehmens. Zusammen mit Dieter Maupai hat er *La Grammaire en s'amusant* (8714) verfaßt und außerdem *La Conversation en s'amusant* (8873) sowie *Sprachen lernen* (60842) geschrieben.

In der Reihe Business English sind von beiden Autoren außerdem erschienen: *Manage in English* (60137), *Better than the Boss* (60138), *How to Phone Effectively* (60139), *Drop Them a Line* (60261, mit Bryan Hemming), *Test Your Management Skills* (60260), *Get Through at Meetings* (60262), *Let's Go International* (60267), *Check Your Language Level* (60268), *Business English from A to Z* (60269, mit Bryan Hemming), *The Way Things Work* (60369), *How to Read the Business Press* (60506), *Small Talk for Big Business* (60439), *Business by Jokes* (60721), *Sell like Hell* (60722), *Master Your Business Phrases* (60725) und *Get to Grips with Company English* (60845).

RENÉ BOSEWITZ / ROBERT KLEINSCHROTH

SPICE UP YOUR SPEECHES

RHETORIK FÜR ALLE GESCHÄFTSANLÄSSE

Rowohlt Taschenbuch Verlag

Originalausgabe
Veröffentlicht im Rowohlt
Taschenbuch Verlag GmbH,
Reinbek bei Hamburg,
März 2000

Umschlaggestaltung Barbara Hanke
(**Illustration** Cathrin Günther)
Layout Birgit Meyer und Alexander Urban
Zeichnungen Christian Mentzel
Satz OCR-A und Stone PostScript,
QuarkXPress 4.04
Gesamtherstellung Clausen & Bosse, Leck
Printed in Germany
ISBN 3 499 60804 9

Inhalt

Wegweiser

Tips and tricks for speakers and communicators

Checklists

Formulas

Vorwort

Wer gut redet, kommt schneller voran. Und sie haben eines gemeinsam, die erfolgreichen Menschen: Sie können ihre Gedanken so ausdrücken, daß sie gehört, verstanden, behalten und in die Tat umgesetzt werden. Darum ist Reden halten eine der wichtigsten Nebensachen im Geschäftsleben, und Reden werden im Zuge der Globalisierung zunehmend auf Englisch gehalten. Nur wer gut redet, kann motivieren, Menschen führen und überzeugen. *Spice up your speeches* will Ihre Kommunikationsfähigkeit verbessern und Ihnen zu mehr Sicherheit und Erfolg auf internationalem Parkett verhelfen.

Die Redekunst setzen erfolgreiche Geschäftsleute nicht nur bei großen Anlässen ein. Sie hilft ihnen auch in Interviews und Besprechungen, bei der Begrüßung von Geschäftspartnern, in Verhandlungen, in Präsentationen und auch im Gespräch mit Einzelpersonen. Wer ein paar geschliffene Worte zum Abschluß eines Geschäftsessens, zur Verabschiedung oder Ehrung eines Kollegen findet, hinterläßt bei seinen Vorgesetzten vielleicht einen nachhaltigeren Eindruck als durch seine tägliche Arbeit, die als selbstverständlich vorausgesetzt wird.

In diesem Buch geht es um die vielen kleinen Redeanlässe des Geschäftsalltags. Dabei werden Ihnen nicht nur die Qualitätsmerkmale guter Reden bewußt, in kurzen abwechslungsreichen Übungen lernen Sie, die Register der Rhetorik zu ziehen.

Nebenbei erweitern Sie auch Ihr *business English* und erwerben die typischen *phrases*, mit denen Sie Ihren Vortrag spicken können. Einprägsame Daumenregeln (*Formulas*), Tips und Tricks (*Speaker's corner*) und praktische Checklisten runden die Kapitel ab.

Auch die Freunde des angelsächsischen Humors sollen wieder voll auf ihre Kosten kommen. Dafür sorgen die vielen, auf das Thema abgestimmten *jokes* und geistreichen Zitate. Ein ausführliches Glossar sorgt dafür, daß Sie alles verstehen werden.

Chapter 1

The installation speech

Mr Dobson (**D**), the former head of Public Relations at Ruver, is transferring to Headquarters in Munich in Germany. The Public Relations department in England has a staff of ten. Mr Dobson is introducing Georg Grosleger (**G**) to the company.

D: (*fade in*) ... and so there are a few things and a few people you have to be careful with.

G: That's the same in any job, isn't it?

D: Well, that may be, but watch out for Mr Pointner. He's your section leader and I'm sorry to say he very much wanted your job. And he's disappointed that a foreigner was imported to do it.

G: I certainly didn't expect that. We're all part of the European Union now, aren't we?

D: That's the theory. I hope I don't get any problems like that in Germany when I move over there.

G: I'm afraid you might. But we've got to try anyway.

D: Right! And that brings me to another point. Next Monday I'd like to formally introduce you to the whole department. I'll call a special meeting if that's okay with you. After that I'll sort of fade out.

G: Monday? That's fine. It'll give me a chance to check out our Pointner and the rest as well.

Food for thought

Why doesn't the fellow who says "I'm no speechmaker"
let it go at that instead of giving a demonstration?
Kin Hubbard

(*) Installing a new man (*)

10 o'clock, Monday morning; noise of talking;
Dobson, knocking a desk with a stapler.

Ladies and Gentlemen, could I have your attention for a minute, please? Thank you. As you all know I'm not a great man for speeches, I'm more for action, more for getting things done. (*Grunting in the background*)

And now things have really been "done". I'm referring to the fact that my person has been transferred to Headquarters over there in the land of the leather trousers and the white sausage. Of course, I'm talking about Bavaria and the centre of the world, Munich.

And, to come to the reason for our gathering here, I have great pleasure in introducing you to the person who is to fill the gap – if gap there will be – after I've gone. He comes to us, not as I might mention, from headquarters. He applied to join us directly and in doing so competed with all the applicants on the open market. If I may say so, a laudable act. Laudable, dear colleagues, especially because it is not easy to come to a foreign place to begin work. We all know these are difficult times, what with rationalisation, automation and globalisation. Ladies and Gentlemen, may I present Georg Grosleger from Germany?

Mr Grosleger has come to us after several years of successful experience in Germany. He is very well recommended. His tasks have included supporting the Board of Management in Munich directly with regard to advertising projects. This was in his capacity as an assistant. Now Georg Grosleger has decided to work on more of his own initiative as head of a department.

Mr Grosleger is coming in the "hot" season, to a hot environment to sit on a hot seat. And all of us involved should try to ensure that it does not become an ejector seat. I'm sure our new colleague can count on the support of all of you.

Well, I'll keep it short. On behalf of all of us, I'd like to wish you, Georg, great success in your new responsibility for the future. It is a difficult task, but we believe that you are the right man to master it.

Working with the language

Task 1: Key words in business

Here are some expressions Dobson used in his speech.
Can you fill in the missing words?

.... leader	*Abteilungsleiter*
move .... to another company	*zu einer anderen Firma wechseln*
check somebody	*jemanden überprüfen*
be .... to Headquarters	*zur Zentrale versetzt sein / werden*
on the .... market	*auf dem freien Markt*
.... to a company	*sich bei einer Firma bewerben*
be well	*bestens empfohlen sein*
work .... more of one's .... initiative	*mit mehr Eigeninitiative arbeiten*
in one's .... as ...	*in seiner Eigenschaft als ...*
.... the Board of Management	*die Geschäftsleitung unterstützen*
somebody's tasks .... among other things	*jemandes Aufgaben sind / bestehen unter anderen aus ...*

Task 2: Thinker's corner

1. How does Dobson characterise himself?
2. Is the beginning of his speech a good one?
3. What is the main idea that Dobson wants to convey?
4. Which phrase tells us that Grosleger will have a hard job?
5. Which phrase suggests that Grosleger has good references?
6. Why did Dobson stress that Grosleger had not come from headquarters?

Task 3: Three ways of saying it

Fill in *my, to, the, in, of* where necessary.

1. I have ..... great pleasure ..... introducing you .... Mr G.
2. I have ..... great pleasure ..... introducing you ..... Mr G.
3. It's ..... pleasure ..... introduce ..... Mr G.

Task 4: Say it the speaker's way

What Dobson might have said, but didn't. Replace the words in *italics*.

1. Could *you be quiet* for a minute?
2. To come to the reason *why we are* here …
3. May I *introduce* Georg Grosleger from Germany?
4. This was in his *job* as an assistant.
5. *In the name* of all of us, I'd like to wish you great success.

(B) Building your speeches

1. Welcome the audience

Ich danke Ihnen, daß Sie heute gekommen sind.	I'd like to thank you for attending today.
Ich freue mich, Sie heute alle begrüßen zu dürfen.	I'm happy to welcome all of you today.
Ich freue mich, Sie anläßlich … bei uns begrüßen zu können.	It's a pleasure / I'm glad to welcome you here on the occasion of …
Im Namen des Unternehmens darf ich Sie herzlich begrüßen.	On behalf of the management allow me to extend a warm welcome to you.
Ich bin Ihnen dankbar, daß Sie eine Stunde Ihrer wertvollen Zeit opfern, um mir zuzuhören.	I appreciate that you're sacrificing one hour of your valuable time to listen to me.

What to say to a small audience

Did you all come in one car?

As only half of the invited guests have come here tonight, I'd really appreciate if you could all applaud twice as loud when I finish.

2. Tell them why you are here

Man hat mich eingeladen, um Ihnen einen Überblick über die Geschichte der Druckmaschinen zu geben. — I have been invited to give you a short history of the world of printing presses.

Um zum Anlaß unserer Zusammenkunft zu kommen, … — To come to the reason for our gathering here, …

Sie sind heute hier zusammengekommen, um etwas über unsere Vorstellung über … zu hören. — Now, you've met here today to hear something about our ideas on …

Wie Sie wissen, bin ich hier, um Ihnen … vorzustellen. — As you know, I'm here to present … to you.

Ich möchte Ihnen einen kurzen Überblick über … geben. — I'd like to give you a brief breakdown of …

Gegenstand meines Vortrags ist … — The topic of my talk is …

Das Thema meiner Rede ist … — The subject of my speech is …

In meiner Präsentation werde ich unser neues Projekt erläutern. — In my presentation I'll be explaining our new project.

Ich freue mich, daß ich die Gelegenheit habe, zu Ihnen über … zu sprechen. — I'm glad to have the chance to speak to you on the subject of …

Vielen Dank, daß Sie mich zum Thema … eingeladen haben. — Thank you for asking me to tell you about …

Ich bin dankbar, daß man mir Gelegenheit gibt, Ihnen unsere Produktpalette vorzustellen. — I'm grateful for having been offered the opportunity to present our product range.

How not to introduce a guest of honour

Ladies and Gentlemen, we are gathered here to pay tribute to a man known to all of us … a man who deserves the praise of every person here tonight … a man who is a shining example of all that is good, a man to whom many of us look for guidance. … But enough about the pope! Let's talk about this man here! … He is something, isn't he?

Ⓢ Spice up your speeches

Figures of speech

As a good speaker you should avoid abstract language. Try to create powerful impressions to make your speech memorable. Instead of a flow of abstract words you use visual language, images, and figures of speech. Figures of speech include images, similes and metaphors and many other "tasty" things. A memorable image can stay in your mind long after you have forgotten the rest of the speech.

- A simile compares two things that are not similar using the linking words "like" and "as": her dreams dried up *like a raisin in the sun*; he is *as hard as rock*.
- A metaphor is an image that does not use these linking words to make the comparison: this woman is *a tower of strength*
- Irony says one thing, but means something else.
  And you don't want to bore your audience, you try to be entertaining. You might spice your speech with a little joke (more about that later), with a play on words or with a little irony.

A word about repetition

Why should a speaker waste time and bore his audience by repeating things over and over again?

1. Repetition is a powerful means to anchor names of products, companies and persons in the memories of the listeners.
2. Repetition serves to emphasise and highlight an idea or an argument. It increases the turnover of words and reduces the turnover of ideas. Thus the audience gets more time to digest the idea.
3. However, repetition word by word is the exception. Variation is the spice of life. Repeat the same thing in other words:
   "I'm more for *action,* more for *getting things done*".

And often the speaker uses repetition to gradually intensify an idea by building up to a climax.

"Mr Grosleger is coming in the *'hot' season,* to a *hot environment* to sit on a *hot seat*".

Task 5: Find the spices

Look at Dobson's speech again and discover examples of

1. metaphor
2. irony
3. word play

Task 6: Watch out for repetition

"Mr Grosleger is coming in the 'hot' season,
to a hot environment to sit on a hot seat".
Dobson has repeated this idea three times in his speech.

Can you find the other three repetitions?

✔ Checkpoint: The installation speech

An installation speech serves two purposes:

A. to explain why the new colleague is qualified for a function
B. to win him or her the support of his/her colleagues

And here's a checklist to help you to write a speech of this type:

1. Say why there is a vacancy to be filled.
2. Thank and praise the candidates who didn't get it – if necessary.
3. Describe the requirements for the job.
4. Don't provide the candidate's entire life story. Instead give examples of the candidates qualities such as experience, judgement, initiative and energy.
5. Link these qualities to aspects of his future activities.
6. Mention his or her name as often as possible.
7. Whip up support for the new colleague.
8. Wish the new man or woman good luck in his future job.

Speaker's corner: A good impression is a matter of minutes

If we lived in a different kind of world, people would *judge* us for our hard work, intelligence and effort. The reality is that many intelligent people who work hard and *keep their heads down* get overlooked: those with a talent for personal public relations get the *rewards*. Successful relationships in our business life *depend on* how we manage our *behaviour* in different situations in order to create an *appropriate* impression.

Research shows that a strong *impression* is made within moments, and a *lasting opinion* based on how we look, *sound* and *move* within half a minute to four minutes. You won't get a second chance to make a good impression. Few of us are free of irrational *prejudice* – men with earrings, women on motorbikes etc.

As a speaker you send out complex information about yourself – who you are and what you stand for. The initial *impact* you create does not depend on what you have to say. It is dominated by what your listeners see: by your outward *appearance*, your dress, gestures and facial expression. Next, they focus on what they can hear; things such as the tone of your voice, your accent and how loudly you speak. Finally, they *focus* on the words themselves. That's how you influence your audience: by word: 10 percent, by voice: 40 percent, by *body language:* 50 percent.

So "don't say anything you can smile, don't smile anything you can wink, don't *wink* anything you can *nod*."

(Earl Long, American politician, 1895–1960)

beurteilen
den Kopf einziehen
Belohnungen
abhängen von
Verhalten
angemessen
Eindruck
feste Meinung
klingen; bewegen
Vorurteil
Wirkung
Erscheinung
sich konzentrieren
Körpersprache
zwinkern
nicken

Chapter 2

Waking up the staff

Georg Grosleger (**G**) has been at Ruver for three weeks on "reconnaissance". He calls a department meeting to take place on July 1st. He is discussing the matter with a member of the Board, Dr Koutert (**K**).

K: I know you're new at Ruver, but nevertheless you've got to take the bull by the horns. You've got problems in Public Relations.

G: Where do you see the most serious problems?

K: Listen, I know your department well. First, you are not pulling together. Too much time is spent talking about minor issues. Next, several of your people are behaving like civil servants who think they can more or less work to rule.

G: That might be true. I've already noticed a certain, well, not laziness, but certainly an attitude of "well, it'll take care of itself".

K: There's something else I wanted to mention. Your second-in-command, Pointner. He's behaving in a negative way. He's …

G: You don't need to mention it. I've already got the message. I'll have to deal with it in the near future.

K: Okay, Georg, that's all I wanted to say. Let's go for it!

How not to start your speech

Before I begin my speech I'd like to warn you
that I'm suffering from a severe handicap
– I'm sober.

(*) The shock therapy method (*)

July 1st. Georg Grosleger is addressing his department.

Ladies and Gentlemen,
First of all, I'd like to thank you all for attending today. I know you've all been busy. However, I feel that we need this meeting because we are at a crossroads.
This crossroads has two possible directions. One direction is to continue as we have, doing what must be done and getting it done – but nothing more. The second direction is to put in a greater investment in time and energy. And to do this with careful and logical preparation so that we can reach our work targets efficiently. And, dear colleagues, these goals must be fulfilled. Jobs depend on it. Our jobs depend on it. As you know we are living in difficult times when keeping well within the budget and achieving department objectives are vitally important. Therefore, I want each individual member of this department to think it over and to opt for the second direction. And he or she must be willing to do what is necessary at full steam – as part of the team.
At present, Ladies and Gentlemen, we are working, perhaps even hard, but we are running around like headless chickens. What did that famous politician, Lenin, once say? "We're taking one step forwards and two steps back".
That was okay in a Leninist society, but we are all on the free market. Our jobs are not guaranteed. And when we don't do our bit, we could be out. Okay, let's imagine we've all seen the danger. What does the future look like? These are the processes I see before us if we want to change things, to survive.
First, we go back to our workplaces and think it through. From the management side we'll arrange for all section leaders to make a description of tasks and functions within their departments. Then we'll prioritise them. And finally draw up a time line.
Section leaders will report to me that milestones are kept to. If they are not, then there could be problems.
Okay, I want to keep it short. It's my job to see that the headless chicken syndrome is eliminated. If it's a question of animals at all, then I'd like

to see a colony of ants, each with his own tasks, but all with a general purpose to the good of the whole. Off to our ant-hill and let's just do it! Or to put it another way, let's forget the chickens. We should spread our wings and fly with eagles. Good luck!
So, Ladies and Gentlemen, that was everything from my side. May I now ask you for comments, contributions and co-operation?

W Working with the language

Task 1: Key words in business

Here are some expressions Georg used in his speech.
Can you fill in the prepositions and the verbs?

be .... a reconnaissance	*auf einer Informations-/ Erkundungsreise sein*
.... a meeting	*eine Besprechung anberaumen*
talk .... minor issues	*über Nebensächliches sprechen*
work .... rule	*Dienst nach Vorschrift machen*
.... work targets	*Arbeitsziele erreichen*
.... goals	*Vorgaben erfüllen/Ziele erreichen*
.... one's objectives	*sein Soll erfüllen/Ziele verwirklichen*
Jobs depend .... it.	*Arbeitsplätze hängen davon ab.*
a description .... functions	*eine Arbeitsplatzbeschreibung*
ask .... co-operation	*um Zusammenarbeit bitten*
make a	*einen Beitrag liefern*

How not to start a speech
I'm here to speak to you.
You are here to listen to me –
if you finish first let me know.

Task 2: Thinker's corner

1. Which image in the speech tells us that there are two possible ways to go forward?
2. What are the two main points that Georg wants to convey?
3. "May I now ask you for *comments, contributions and co-operation*?" What is this figure of speech called? What effect does it produce?
4. Find the phrases where George indicates they might lose their jobs.
5. In the last paragraph there are several references to the animal kingdom. What impressions does Georg want to create?
   A. produce a surprise effect
   B. show indirectly that he wants them to work systematically as a team
   C. create a stylistic effect
   D. use indirect criticism

Task 3: Three ways of saying it

George's variations of the theme "Ziele erreichen"

1. A.........ing department o.......... is vitally important.
2. We have to .... our work t.......... efficiently.
3. These g......... must be f.................

Task 4: Say it the speaker's way

What Georg might have said, but didn't.

1. I *think* that we need this meeting because we *have to take a decision*.
2. I'*d like* each member of this department to *choose* the second direction.
3. And when we don't do *what we have to do*, we could be out.
4. And he or she must be willing to *carry out* what is necessary at full steam.
5. Then we'll *set priorities*. And finally *fix* a time line.

Task 5: Say it with an image.

1. We do not work systematically and efficiently.
2. We are falling behind our work targets.
3. Do what is necessary at full power.
4. I'd like to see more co-operation and teamwork.
5. Back to our work.
6. Let's use our talents and be among the best.
7. Work goals and dates have to be kept.

(B) Building your speeches

Five effective speech openers

1. The shock tactic introduction

Georg wanted to shock and provoke in order to wake up a department that had fallen into a comfortable habit of taking things too easy. Careful! You have to know your audience well enough to calculate the risks of this method. He could also have started like this:

Ladies and Gentlemen, there is a rumour that HQ will introduce lean management and might lay off 1,500 employees.

2. The "That's-me-opening"

What to do if there is no host to introduce you or if he has forgotten to do so? Use the "That's me" opening and project a photo of a baby:

That's me when I took my first degree. Let me tell you a bit about this baby.

3. The rhetorical question

It is one of the easiest, most common and most effective ways to open a speech. It creates a link between you and the listeners. It involves them because they immediately begin to frame an answer, and then listen closely to see if their answer matches yours. Georg could have started like this:

What can we compare this department to? A chicken yard, an ant-hill? A yard of chickens running around in all directions? Or a colony of ants, each with his own tasks, but responsible for and dedicated to the good of the community?

4. The story

Imagine you had to speak before a group of marketing or sales people. Wouldn't this story be a good start to illustrate how difficult it can be to recognise sales opportunities?

Two shoe salesmen travelled on the same boat to West Africa, each representing different shoe companies. After landing they looked around, and what struck them first was the fact that all the natives were barefoot.

The first salesman cabled his head office: "Nobody here wearing shoes. Coming home by next ship."

The second salesman cabled his boss: "Nobody here wearing shoes. Market is wide open."

5. The Anecdote

The following story could be used as an opening in a training seminar. Receptionists, waiters and policemen tend to judge people by their appearance, which can be a mistake – as this story illustrates:

One day, a shabby gentleman turned up at the National Gallery with a painting under his arm. He asked to see the director, but was rudely turned away, and only after he had waited patiently and repeated his request was he allowed in.

The old man tried to persuade the director to take a quick look, but he firmly refused and was on the verge of having him removed from the office when the covering fell off – revealing a masterpiece that the director had tried but failed to buy at an auction.

"My name is Sir William Wallace," said the shabby gentleman, a well known millionaire, quietly, "I came to offer this picture to the National Gallery."

You will find another five speech openers in chapter 13.

Checkpoint: The opening of the speech

Whatever opening you choose, you should ask yourself whether it accomplishes the following tasks:

1. Does it forge a bond with the audience?
2. Does it establish credibility and goodwill?
3. Does it create interest?
4. Does it catch attention?
5. Does it announce the theme?

Speaker's corner: Know your audience

Is your audience the kind that will *appreciate* the story of your life or will they respond to a more general joke about business? One of the first things to *bear in mind* is the kind of material they'll enjoy.
Contact the organiser of the *event* and find out if there is anything special or interesting about the *occasion*. Is the society, club or organisation involved in anything new or exciting? If it is, *make reference* to the fact in your speech and try to find some quotations or stories to build round it. This can be hard work, but it shows that you've done your *research* and that you care for your *audience*. They will love any stories you can come up with, and your *success* will be guaranteed.

- Collect all the information you can get about the *participants*. Find out what kind of *mood* the audience will be in and what will please them in that mood.
- *Consider* their age. The over-sixties will enjoy nostalgic humour with lots of references to

schätzen
denken an
Ereignis
Anlaß
Bezug nehmen
Recherchen; Zuhörer
Erfolg
Teilnehmer; Stimmung
berücksichtigen

their younger days, while a group of young intellectuals will prefer something sharper and more informative.

- The *sex* of the audience will *affect* their response. Jokes about secretaries and office scandals will find favour with an *all-male gathering*, but probably won't go down so well in mixed company.
- *Bear* all this *in mind* when you come to select your material. It may sound *obvious*, but many a good speech has been ruined by the choice of an *inappropriate* line.

Geschlecht; beeinflussen
Männergesellschaft
denken an
selbstverständlich
unpassend

Chapter 3

The keystone speech

Dr Mayer (**M**), the Board member responsible for finance, has fixed in his large and luxurious office an appointment with Georg (**G**). It's the first time that Georg has met such a "high animal". He wants to create a good impression.

M: Do sit down, Mr Grosleger. Well, how are you settling in? I suppose we all look a bit chaotic compared with your previous employer over there in Germany.

G: Not at all, not at all! Actually things seem to be going on in a relaxed way, but nevertheless people are really getting things done.

M: I'm glad to hear that. To the point, Mr Grosleger, I need your support. I have to make a keystone speech. Ruver is going to lay the foundation stone of our new training centre in Manchester. It'll be called the Academy for the World of Cars.

G: A terrific name, if I may say so,

M: And you should prepare my speech. I know you're not a native speaker even though you've got an excellent knowledge of English. But you know what's got to be in there. Get somebody from the marketing department to edit it. I have full confidence in you.

Time for a smile

"Why did you walk out in the middle of my speech?" asked the company Chairman one of his senior executives. "It was an important meeting of the shareholders and you chose the most crucial moment to walk out, when I had been speaking for only forty minutes."

"I'm sorry, sir," replied the senior executive, "but it was nothing personal. I was just sleepwalking."

(*) Laying a foundation stone (*)

Dr Mayer at the Academy of the World of Cars.

Very Honourable Members of Parliament, Lord Mayor,
Ladies and Gentlemen, Dear Colleagues,

First of all I'd like to thank you for spending some of your valuable time to visit this very special event for our company. And I'd like to start by expressing my gratitude to the municipal authorities, especially our esteemed Lord Mayor for his advice and support.
And I want to add a hearty "thank-you" to the men and women here, our most valuable asset, to whom we owe this solemn moment. Because of your good work, whether in assembly, purchasing, sales or marketing, or any of the support services, you have all pulled together in the Ruver boat to bring us upstream and through the rapids of competition and rules and regulations.
And now to the reason for our being together today. Ruver has had problems in the past, but it has struggled through to become, perhaps not the market leader, but in our own area a little giant, a conservative company in the best meaning of the word, but progressive and flexible at the same time.
One of the results is this Academy of the World of Cars. On my left you see the entrance area open to the world, on my right, at the end of the academy, a showroom where our history appears in the form of our most successful and even less successful cars from the past. What is this academy about? The answer, my friends, is communication. People in our sector, whether customers or staff, everyone in our sector, has a centre, a place where there is an exchange of know-how, of information. Here, visitors can get training and advice, can learn more about our field of business and our technology in general. And so, Ladies and Gentlemen, it stands here in front of us, an academy, a possibility to learn more about our business. It is at the same time a visiting card for our activities in the field of the automotive industry. And, if I may mention it, the Academy is a real innovation, the first of its type in the world.

And so I come to the climax of our gathering here. It is with great pleasure that I cement this keystone into place. (*Scraping a trowel on stone*). Let us hope these stones will be bound together into an institution which is more than simply brick and mortar. That it will stand in the world as a foundation of knowledge and progressive thinking. With this act I wish the Academy and Ruver in general success in their enterprises. All the best!

And now to finish. As it has been said before: "If you stand up, you'll be seen. If you speak up, you'll be heard. If you sit down, you'll be appreciated." Having said that, I'll sit down and allow us to partake of some refreshments.

Working with the language

Task 1: Key words in business

Here are some phrases they have used in dialogue and speech. Can you fill in the missing words?

.... in a company	*sich in eine Firma eingewöhnen*
.... someone's support	*jemandes Unterstützung benötigen*
.... a speech	*eine Rede überarbeiten*
.... together	*am gleichen Strang ziehen*
.... one's work done	*seine Arbeit erledigen*
.... the market leader	*Marktführer werden*
.... of know-how	*Austausch von Fachwissen*
be .... in the .... of the automotive business	*auf dem Gebiet der Automobilindustrie tätig sein*

Lack of preparation

A certain literary society had advertised a talk on the great poet Keats and at the last moment had asked the mayor, a well-meaning but ignorant man, to take the chair and introduce the guest speaker. After a few remarks on the occasion he concluded by saying: "Now, I'm sure you're all as anxious as I am for the speaker to begin and let us know, just exactly what keats are".

Task 2: Thinker's corner

1. What does Dr Mayer intend by addressing the workforce?
   A. To thank the workforce?
   B. To create a sense of community and shared values?
   C. To talk about past difficulties and present achievements?
2. What does he speak about in the fourth paragraph?
3. How does he appeal to the audience to use their imagination?
4. What does Dr Mayer say to lighten the atmosphere and bring things to a close?

Task 3: The structure of speeches

Dr Mayer structured his speech with those little words: *first, second, next, and then* etc. Remember how Dr Mayer did it?

1. .... I'd like to thank you for spending some of your valuable time to ...
2. .... a hearty "thank-you" to the men and women here.
3. .... the reason for our being together today.
4. .... the climax of our gathering here.
5. .... finish.

Task 4: Say it the speaker's way

Finding more concrete phrases! Do it Dr Mayer's way.

1. And so I come to the climax of our *reunion* here.
2. It is with great pleasure that I *lay the foundation stone.*
3. What is *the function of* this academy?
4. Ruver has had problems in the past, but it has *tried to solve them.*

Time for a smile

Friend: You received a tremendous ovation. In fact, they're still clapping. What did you say?

Speaker: I told them I would not go on with my speech until they quietened down.

Ⓢ Spice up your speeches

All speeches consist of information and ornaments. What is an ornament and why is it necessary? Ornaments add beauty and elegance to your speech. If you don't decorate it with appropriate figures of speech like imagery, repetition and examples, your listeners will be unable to follow and remember it – and they will be bored. Let's find out how it has been done in this speech.

Task 5: Find the spices

What figures of speech are used to give the idea of

1. the staff's successful co-operation and teamwork,
2. Ruver's past problems and difficulties,
3. the importance of the academy for Ruver's image,
4. building up a solid institution of knowledge for the future,
5. Ruver being a company of considerable importance.

✔ Checkpoint: The opening speech

The keystone speech belongs to the type of speeches that is delivered on special formal occasions like celebrations, anniversaries or openings of buildings. Here's a checklist to help you to write a speech of this type:

1. Compliment entry: Greet the audience, address the honorary guests by their names and titles.
2. Create a feeling of belonging, of shared values and common interests.
3. Explain why you have come together.
4. Give a short historical overview of what you have achieved together.
5. Give an optimistic outlook to the future.

Speaker's corner: Speeches for special occasions

A formal entertaining speech is held on *occasions* like ribbon cuttings, keystone layings and other *inaugurations*. If your director asks you to deliver the opening speech at the annual sales *convention* and you read the sales report as your speech, you haven't fulfilled the *purpose*. The intention of this type of speech is to

Anlässe
Einweihung
Kongreß
Zweck

- *entertain* the audience
- *set* the right atmosphere
- draw people together into a community by creating a feeling of *belonging*.

unterhalten
schaffen
Zusammengehörigkeit

What to do

To *accomplish* this aim, you will have to

- talk about the *aims* you have *achieved* together
- go for emotional *appeals* and personal identification
- *appeal* to the interests and values you share with the audience
- be optimistic about the future
- use elegant speech and *ornaments*
- be short

verwirklichen
Ziele; erreichen
Appelle
ansprechen
Verzierungen

What to *avoid*

- Don't talk about yourself.
- Don't appeal to *reason* and logic.
- Don't be provocative.
- Don't try to be too funny.
- Don't read your speech from your notes.

vermeiden

Vernunft

Chapter 4

The Annual General Meeting

Georg Grosleger (**G**) is sitting in the office of Dr Naston (**N**), Chairman of the Board of Ruver P.L.C. It's a very big office, the desk is made of reddish marble.

N: I don't know what the practice is in Germany, but here in England the Chairman of the Board has to make a short speech.
G: Well, we have it in Germany, too, but I guess a short speech means two or three hours.
N: Oh, my goodness, no! Keep in mind that I don't want to speak for more than eight or ten minutes. Remember time is money.
G: Could you give me the key ideas so I can construct it accurately?
N: Of course, that's why I called you up today. First, I'd like to start by mentioning a couple of personal points. Mr John Cardet, director of research died last week. The second point is that Dr Koutert, director of development, will be promoted to the Board. In addition to these issues I'll be including last year's trading, dividend, share capital, volume of business etc. Here's the data. When you've prepared everything, a copy to me for the final check. Okay, Mr Grosleger, keep up the good work!

What to say about a dead colleague

To the distinguished audience:
You can't control the length of your life, but you can control its breadth, depth and height.

To a cool audience:
What an organiser John Cardert was! If he'd been running this funeral, we'd all have been down at the pub by now.

⊛ Eulogies and facts and figures ⊛

Gentlemen,

Welcome to our Annual General Meeting. Before we proceed to the business of this meeting, I have two matters of personal interest to mention. The first is a sad one. I must remind you of the loss we have sustained through the passing away of Mr John Cardet. Mr Cardet was one of our oldest Directors, and he served us well in good times and bad. We shall feel the loss of his wise counsel and shrewd foresight; and still more, we shall miss a loyal and sincere friend. On this occasion I should like to record our deep sympathy for his family. (*Pause*)

The other personal matter to which I must draw your attention is of a happier kind. It is that Dr Koutert, who has been a director for six years, has climbed the weary path to the Board. I am sure that you will want me, on behalf of the meeting, to congratulate Dr Koutert most warmly. Working in the Board requires general management skills. However, Dr Koutert will continue in his capacity as head of development. He will continue to be an engineer and will give us all the benefit of his considerable experience and ability.

And now to those impersonal figures. Last year's trading – as you will see from the handouts before you – was a relief to us all from every point of view. Our net profits amounted to £20 million which represents an increase of £5 million on the previous year. Provision for taxation required £50 million (as compared with £40 million the previous year). With the amount brought forward there is available for distribution the sum of £ 30 million. A final dividend of 50 per cent, making 65 per cent (less tax) on Ordinary Share Capital is proposed. This will absorb £10 million. After appropriations the carry forward is £8 million. Our total reserves, including capital reserves, now amount to £80 million. This represents an increase of £15 million.

You will see that the volume of our business has risen by over 20 per cent. It is difficult to forecast business conditions in the coming year, but provided that the supply of raw materials is undisturbed, and that prices remain at their present level, there is every reason to believe that our profits will be at least maintained and possibly increased.

During the last year much modernisation has been carried out, and in

spite of the considerable expense it is our feeling that this has already proved an excellent investment. Further modernisation is still in the pipeline, and it is our intention to continue this policy as circumstances permit.
Our employees now number 4,500. Rumours that we are thinking of streamlining the company are unfounded. Apart from the normal replacements, there have been comparatively few changes of staff during the year. We give a lot of thought to the well being of our staff. There is a healthy team spirit among the employees of the company, and I am sure you will wish to join with me in expressing our appreciation of the devotion and loyalty of our staff. Let's stride forward into the future together.

Working with the language

Task 1: Key words in business

Can you complete the language of meetings?

.... to the Board	*in den Vorstand befördern*
.... the good work	*weiterhin so gut arbeiten*
.... to the business of the meeting	*zum Gegenstand der Besprechung schreiten*
.... a matter of personal interest	*etwas Persönliches erwähnen*
.... somebody's attention to	*jemanden aufmerksam machen auf*
.... in one's capacity as head of development	*weiterhin in seiner Eigenschaft als Leiter der Entwicklung tätig sein*
.... someone the .... of one's experience	*jemandem seine Erfahrung zukommen lassen*
.... business conditions in the coming year	*die Geschäftsbedingungen des nächsten Jahres voraussagen*
the .... of raw materials is	*der Nachschub an Rohmaterial läuft störungsfrei*

Task 2: Let money speak

Same procedure as before.

net profits .... to ...	*die Nettogewinne belaufen sich auf*
.... an increase of ... on the previous year	*einen Anstieg von ... gegenüber dem letzten Jahr darstellen*
.... an amount of ...	*einen Betrag von ... verschlingen*
.... a dividend of ...	*eine Dividende in Höhe von ... vorschlagen*
prices .... at their present level	*Preise halten sich auf dem gegenwärtigen Stand*
profits will be	*Gewinne werden aufrechterhalten*
.... a good investment	*sich als gute Investition erweisen*
the volume of business has .... by 20 per cent	*das Geschäftsvolumen ist um 20 Prozent gestiegen*

Task 3: Thinker's corner

1. How many major sections is this speech divided into?
2. What are the themes of these sections?
3. Can you identify the two different styles of speech Dr Naston uses?
4. In the first two paragraphs one stylistic feature is repeated several times. Which? What effect does it produce?

Task 4: Polish up your English

Dr Naston used a more elegant way of saying these things.

1. I must remind you *that we have suffered a loss.*
2. I have two *personal matters to mention.*
3. The other personal matter *is a happier one.*
4. It is our intention to continue this policy *as well as possible.*

(B) Building your speeches

Phrases for speakers

This is how Dr Naston expressed his certainty about things:

"*I am sure that* you will want me to congratulate Dr Koutert most warmly.
There is every reason to believe that our profits will be maintained ..."

Since variety is the spice of life here are some phrases to choose from.

Expressing certainty

Ich bin überzeugt, daß ...	I'm convinced that ...
Ich bin zuversichtlich, daß ...	I'm (quite) confident (that)...
Ich bin absolut sicher, daß ...	I'm (absolutely) certain (that)...
Es ist völlig klar, daß ...	It's (quite / absolutely) clear (that)...
Es ist meine feste Überzeugung, daß ...	It's my (firm) belief / conviction (that)...
Ich glaube fest, daß ...	I firmly believe (that)...
Es ist meine ehrliche Überzeugung, daß ...	I sincerely believe *(that)...*
Ich habe keinerlei Zweifel, ...	There is / can be no doubt ...
Es gibt nicht den geringsten Zweifel, daß ...	There is not a shadow of doubt that ...

A convincing argument

A lawyer is addressing an all-male jury: "Gentlemen, shall we cast this beautiful young lady into a dark, dim cell, or shall we return her to her lovely apartment on Park Avenue, telephone 555-6969?"

Use an outline

Why bother with an outline? First, it helps you to see whether you have forgotten an item. Second, it shows you whether you have arranged the main ideas in the best possible way. Third, it helps you to memorise your speech. This is Dr Naston's outline of his speech:

A. Personal matters
- **1.** Death of Mr Cardet
- **2.** Promotion of Dr Koutert

B. Business matters
- **1.** Refer to handouts
- **2.** Overview of last year's results
- **3.** Outlook for the future

C. Personnel matters
- **1.** Changes of staff
- **2.** Working climate

Make your style suit your theme

Dr Naston used two forms of speech which differ in style. Remembering a colleague who has died and congratulating a colleague who has been promoted belong to the entertaining type (even if the occasion is a sad one). Style, atmosphere and ornament are more important than information. He appeals to emotions rather than to logic.

Part B and C are informative. Dr Naston presents facts and figures in short and precise sentences. By the way, the audience wouldn't have been able to follow, if Naston hadn't distributed a handout or used an overhead projector.

Advice from the expert

A speech is like a love affair. Any fool can start it,
but to end it requires considerable skill.
Lord Mancroft

Ⓢ Spice up your speeches

Figures of speech

A **euphemism** is an expression that is gentler or less direct than the one normally used to refer to something unpleasant or embarrassing.

Task 5: Find the spices

Dr Naston used figures of speech to express the following ideas. Can you do it?

1. Dr Koutert has worked himself up to the Board the hard way.
2. Mr John Cardet has died.
3. Modernisation is still being prepared or discussed.
4. Rumours that we will fire employees are unfounded.

Task 6: Say it the speaker's way

Dr Naston added rhythm and weight to his sentences by using two words of similar meaning instead of one. Do you remember?

1. Mr John Cardet *always* served us well.
2. We feel the loss of Mr Cardet's *support*.
3. And still more, we shall miss a *good friend*.
4. Dr Koutert will give us all the benefit of his considerable *know-how*.
5. We appreciate the *faithfulness* of our staff.

Advice from the expert

A speech is like a woman's skirt.
It should be long enough to cover the subject,
but short enough to make it interesting.

A good speech is like a well-kept lawn: short and neat.

✔ Checkpoint: Everything under control?

The successful speaker's checklist

Be prepared

1. Do I know my audience?
   Who are they? What do they expect?
2. What do I expect them to remember or do?
3. Have I got a clear outline of my speech?
4. Is it clearly structured?
5. Have I cut out all the less important facts?
6. Have I included enough examples to support my arguments?
7. Shall I use OHP, Flipchart, video recorder, handouts etc?
8. Do I have a provocative, ironic opening to my speech?
9. How will I end my speech?
10. How do I dress for success? Are my clothes adapted to the age and position of my listeners?

Good intentions

1. I'll try to identify with my audience.
2. I won't speak too fast.
3. I won't read my speech.
4. I'll speak loudly and clearly.
5. I'll keep my body language under control.
6. I'll remember the pauses where necessary.
7. I'll keep eye contact with my audience.
8. I won't let them provoke me.
9. I'll answer even the most stupid question politely.
10. I'll think positive and be optimistic whatever happens.

Last minute check at the set

1. Do I need a microphone? If yes, adjust the volume.
2. Should I use the rostrum or not?
3. Can everybody see me?
4. Does the OHP and the video function properly?
5. Can everybody see the screen?

Speaker's corner: Speaking to inform

The informative speech *appeals* to logic and reason. Your task is to help your listeners to understand the *essential* ideas you present.

The *purpose* of your speech might be to
- explain plans or a strategies
- report the department's results
- describe a process or the plan of a factory
- *propose* solutions and alternatives
- define *targets*
- present products
- train the staff
- demonstrate *devices* in action

sich wenden an
wesentlich
Zweck, Ziel
vorschlagen
Ziele
Geräte

Know your audience

The more clearly your speech is organised, the better they will remember it. *Link* your ideas to what they already know about the *subject*. Give them examples, if they are not *familiar* with the theme.

verbinden
Gegenstand
vertraut

Structure it

First give them an *overview* of your speech. There are several ways to structure it. If you talk about problems, explain the causes, show the effects and offer *solutions*. If you describe a process, do it in chronological order: first – then – next.

Überblick
Lösungen

Visualise it

You must show whatever is difficult to explain in words. Use the flipchart, the *OHP* or *slides*.

Overheadprojektor; Dias

When in *doubt*, leave out

Zweifel

The problem with experts is that they know too much and tend to *overload* their talk with details and technical terms. *Knock out* what you cannot illustrate or visualise with examples. And don't write more on a *transparency* or flipchart than you would on a T-shirt.

überladen
rauswerfen
Folie

Chapter 5

The spontaneous speech

Georg (**G**) is sitting in his office when the phone rings. It is Bryan Cahill (**C**), the department leader of the new Ruver off-roader series.

G: Grosleger speaking. How can I help you?

C: Hello, my name's Cahill from the off-roader division. I'd like to request your help. Next week on Friday we'll be having the annual executive dinner. The personnel director has just told me they'll be calling on me to make a "spontaneous" speech to the prosperity of the company. A speech directed towards the Board of Management.

G: And, of course, you've got to make sure you sound appreciative and sincere. You mustn't simply flatter the bosses or it'll go down like a stone.

C: Yes, and everybody would be embarrassed and I'd suffer later.

G: It's got to be managed with healthy appreciation and good balance. Can you send me an e-mail with all the points you want to include and we'll see what we can do?

Successful Spontaneous Speakers

I am the most spontaneous speaker in the world
because every word, every gesture, and every retort
has been carefully rehearsed.
G.B. Shaw

It normally takes me more than three hours to prepare
a good spontaneous speech.
Mark Twain

(*) The prosperity of the company (*)

Mr Chairman, Ladies and Gentlemen, Dear Colleagues,
I can say in all sincerity that I am very pleased to have the honour of proposing the toast to the company. Winston Churchill once said that there were only two things that are more difficult than making an after-dinner speech: climbing a wall which is leaning towards you and kissing a girl who is leaning away from you.
But the thing that makes it so easy and, indeed, pleasurable a task is simply that it is out of office hours. The company is, at the moment, a sort of *illusion*. Seeing all my colleagues here without their copiers and mobile phones, computers, and dining and wining so well, makes me forget the tiring realities of business life. Only for the moment, of course. Now, if you had called on me to propose the health of the company at four o'clock this afternoon, or if you were to ask me to do it at nine o'clock tomorrow morning, I should say I'd rather climb a g... (*chuckling among the audience*) ... ehm ... a wall that is leaning away from me ... Well, never mind what I would say. In any case that's no comment on the company.
I have been with the company for twenty years. I expect to be here another twenty – I thank you for accepting that threat. In total that will be forty years. Now I ask you, why should I spend nearly the whole of my working life in the service of one company? There are only two possible answers. The obvious one, of course, is that I might not get another job. The other answer, which I greatly prefer, is that I can't imagine working for a different company. I like it here.
I'm not going to pretend that I'm one of those rare birds who live for their work. I work for my living. But as working hours make up quite a large proportion of living hours, it seems important that one should be satisfied in one's job. And that satisfaction, very largely, depends on one's company. I think this is a well run company. I like the atmosphere, I like my colleagues, and – believe it or not – I even like our superiors. I think that I have a stake in the company.
Well, I feel my time has elapsed, so I will end by closing in a way you'll all like – by closing my mouth! Ladies and Gentlemen, I ask you to join me in drinking to its continued prosperity. The company!

Ⓦ Working with the language

Task 1: Key words in business

Again something for you to fill in.

.... someone's help	*jemandes Hilfe erbitten*
the .... executive dinner	*das alljährliche Essen der leitenden Angestellten*
.... someone to do something	*jemanden auffordern, etwas zu tun*
.... a speech .... someone	*eine Rede an jemanden richten*
.... one's working life in the .... of one company	*seine Arbeitsjahre im Dienste einer Firma verbringen*
have a .... in the company	*Anteil an der Firma haben / nehmen*
.... of .... hours	*außerhalb der Arbeitszeit*
work .... one's	*für seinen Lebensunterhalt arbeiten*
.... a company	*eine Firma führen / leiten*

Task 2: Thinker's corner

1. How does Bryan create a light, positive atmosphere in the early part of the speech?
2. What image does Bryan use about himself to make it clear that there are more important things than work?
3. Can you explain what rhetorical effect is obtained by "Now I ask you, why should I spend ...?"
4. How does he announce the end of his speech?

Opening an after-dinner speech

I must say, it's always a pleasure to be in the company of civilised and intelligent people.
But of course, I also enjoy evenings like this.

Task 3: Polite noises for speakers

Translate the German expressions.

1. I can say in all .... that I am very pleased to have the .... of proposing the toast to the Company.
2. But the fact that makes it such an easy and, indeed, ... a .... is simply that it is out of office hours.
3. I'm not going to .... that I'm one of those .... birds who live for their work.
4. I ask you to .... me in drinking to the Company's continued ....

Offenheit
Ehre
freudig; Aufgabe
so tun als ob
selten
sich anschließen
Wohlergehen

Ⓑ Building your speeches

Task 4: Create your own toasts

Fit in these verbs and nouns to complete the toasts.

verbs: *propose; raise; celebrate; suggest; toast; rise*
nouns: *agreement; future; toast; conclusion*

1. Let's .... our glasses to the .... of our company.
2. I .... to .... the guests of our company.
3. I'd like to .... a .... to the .... of our contract.
4. I'd like to .... a toast to the company.
5. Let's .... our .... with a glass of champagne.

Advice from the expert
You don't say "Cheers" when you drink a cup of tea in the jungle; you say "Christ, the flies!"
Prince Charles

Ⓢ Spice up your speeches

Special effects

Zeugma: A zeugma is unexpected and creates surprise. You create a zeugma when you use one word that refers to two unexpected words which don't fit together.

She had *flashing* eyes. And
I have a *headache* and a *visitor*.

Freudian slip: It is a comment made accidentally by a speaker instead of what he originally intended to say, but which is considered to reveal his or her true thoughts.

I'm convinced that Mr Dobson is our most
loyal enemy (instead of *loyal friend*).

Some speakers plan such slips to create a humorous effect.

Irony is used when you say the direct opposite of what you are thinking, but using tone of voice to indicate one's real meaning. Irony can be humorous or can give special emphasis to something. It is safer to use irony against oneself rather than against other people

"That's *really lovely*, that is!"
he said with heavy irony. (meaning it's not lovely at all)

Anaphora or parallelism: It is the repetition of a group of words to emphasise one's ideas, the most powerful of which is placed at the end (**climax**).

It was the best of times, *it was the* worst of times,
it was the age of wisdom, *it was the age* of foolishness.

Speakers often combine two figures of speech. The above quotations also contain two examples of paradox.

Task 5: Find the spices

All four figures of speech have been used by Bryan.
Can you complete and identify them?

1. But I see that my time has elapsed, so I will end by ....
2. I expect to be here another twenty years – I thank you for ....
3. I should say I'd rather ....
4. Where did Bryan use parallelism towards the end of his speech?

Checkpoint: Speaking to entertain

Checklist for entertainers

1. Did you observe the "Three-S-rule": Keep it short, sweet, simple?
2. Did you develop your speech around one or two uncomplicated points that the audience can easily grasp?
   Bryan's points: **A.** the atmosphere, **B.** the company
3. How will you create atmosphere?
4. Is your speech personal and will they like your person for it?
5. Is your speech entertaining? Can you include anecdotes from your own personal experience?

Problems

1. If there is no host to introduce you, you'll have two problems.
   - When is the right moment to take the floor? You might interrupt lively conversations and kill the atmosphere.
   - How can you catch the audience's attention? By tapping your glass and shouting: "Can I have your attention please?" or asking a friend to announce and introduce your speech?
2. How can you make your speech personal without talking too much about yourself?
   - Tell them about your impressions and feelings.
   - Catch the atmosphere of the moment and express it.

Speaker's corner: Speeches for informal occasions

Not all speeches deal with "big" *issues*. There are occasions which fulfil the social *need* of bringing people together such as club meetings, house warming and dinner parties, anniversaries or weddings. Speeches *delivered* at these *events* want to

Themen
Bedürfnis
(eine Rede) halten;
Ereignis

- entertain the audience
- create a *relaxed* atmosphere
- *promote* a feeling of social unity that draws people together into a community

entspannt
fördern

These speeches often take a more personal *approach*. However, this is not the time to share your personal problems, paint a *gloomy* picture of the present, or offer pessimistic *predictions* for the future.

Vorgehensweise, Methode
düster
Vorhersagen

If you don't know how to *structure* it, look back to the person's or company's past, talk about their present situation and give an outlook to the future. And if you don't know how to fill the structure, interview people who are *familiar* with the subject. Ask them for anecdotes about the bride, the *guest of honour* or an episode in the company's history.

gliedern
vertraut
Ehrengast

Interestingly, speeches that entertain will often have a more *immediate* effect on your career than speeches with a more serious *purpose*. That's because social occasions often present rich *opportunities* for you to *score points* with the audience. Those points are often cashed in for money and goodwill with business contacts and *influential acquaintances*.

unmittelbar, direkt
Ziel, Zweck
Gelegenheit
Punkte sammeln
einflußreiche Bekannte

Chapter 6

A pep talk

Dr Koutert (**K**), Board Member for Development, Dr Mayer (Finance) and Dr Naston (**N**), Chairman of the Board, are all present at the annual executive dinner.

K: Well, I'm pretty new to this. Which of us should normally reply to this employees' speech on prosperity of the company?

N: Under normal circumstances it wouldn't matter, but since we have done so much restructuring this year, I think I should take the helm in this matter. I'm afraid I'll have to speak off the cuff.

Time for a smile

The chairman of a large company always asked his elderly secretary to write speeches for him. Although the speeches were normally a great success, he never congratulated her on her job. Shortly before she was going to retire, her boss asked her for a speech he was going to make at a conference attended by computer experts.

Everything went smoothly for the first ten minutes. It was a brilliant speech full of hard facts, amusing jokes and snappy quotations that suited the occasion. When the chairman turned the third page of his manuscript he went pale. An awkward silence followed. He read in big letters:

FROM NOW ON YOU ARE ON YOUR OWN, YOU OLD BASTARD.

(*) Reply to the prosperity of the company speech (*)

Ladies and Gentlemen,
I am honoured to reply to the toast of the prosperity of the company, which has been so generously proposed and so genuinely received. This reality alone is, I think, the safest assurance of our future well-being. The success of every organisation, commercial or otherwise, depends primarily on the co-operation of those who run it, and there is no substitute for good relations and teamwork. The same is true for our company.
So when I thank you for the toast I must thank you also for all that you have done for the company in the last twelve months. I hope you will always think of this ... (*Pause*) ... ship not as "it", but as "us". The fact is that every one of us here tonight has a real stake in it. (*Pause*)
I am not going to talk shop on an occasion like this, but I do want to remind you once again of a matter of internal policy which is very dear to our hearts. Each member of the Ruver team has his own job to do, and although we should interact as far as possible, our activities are too complicated to allow us to play musical chairs. But we do want to stimulate your motivation, not only for your own particular job, but for the work of the Ruver as a whole; and more than anything else we want your ideas and suggestions for raising our general efficiency even above its present high level. I believe that there is nothing so destructive to motivation and enthusiasm as a feeling that initiative is not wanted. I assure you that it is desired and needed here, and that the ideas of the most junior members of the staff are not only really welcomed, but will always be treated with the consideration and respect they deserve.
That brings me back to teamwork. I think a good company should be like a good cricket team – all working together for the common good, but aiming at quality and equality of performance at the highest level. We are all, still, individuals with our own particular abilities, and I think that individuality should always be supported within the framework of the team.
Finally, I have pleasure in announcing that as from today our bonus scheme will be restructured in the following way. Every executive will

participate in the company's shares. There will be a Christmas bonus so that in total all executives will receive thirteen and a half salaries. Finally, there will be a success bonus fixed as a percentage. You may also be pleased to hear that the works restaurant will be enlarged.
On behalf of Ruver, Ladies and Gentlemen, I thank you.

The bonus scheme
Here's a joke Mr Naston intended to build into his speech, but didn't. Guess why?

A friend of mine once worked for a company where they had a bonus scheme. After six months they told him that he owed the company money.
Phyllis Diller

W Working with the language

Task 1: Key words in business

Some expressions used in the speech for you to complete.

talk	*fachsimpeln, über die Arbeit reden*
take the	*die Führung übernehmen*
work ...... the ...... of the team	*im Rahmen des Teams arbeiten*
no .... teamwork	*kein Ersatz für Teamarbeit*
have a .... the company	*Anteil nehmen an der Firma*
work ..... for the .... good	*für das allgemeine Wohl arbeiten*
efficiency .... a high	*Leistung auf hohem Niveau*
.... the restaurant	*das Restaurant vergrößern*
.... motivation	*Motivation wecken*
.... the bonus scheme	*das Prämiensystem reorganisieren*
.... co-operation	*auf Kooperation angewiesen sein*
suggestions for .... efficiency	*Vorschläge, um die Leistung zu steigern*

Task 2: Thinker's corner

1. What is the keynote of the introduction of the reply?
2. Find a key word which summarises the main theme of the speech.
3. What does he compare the team to? Why?

Task 3: Say it the speaker's way

1. I'll have to do it *without preparation.*	I'll have to do it ..... the ......
2. We all have an *interest* in the company.	We all have a ..... in the company.
3. I'll take the helm in this matter.	I'll take ..... in this matter.
4. *In the name* of Ruver, I thank you.	.... *of Ruver,* I thank you.

(B) Building your speeches

Use the Three-T-Formula

If you want to entertain or persuade,
develop just one or two themes.

1. The beginning: Tell them what you're going to say.
2. The middle: Tell them what you have to say.
3. The end: Tell them what you have said.

Don't be afraid of repeating yourself
as long as you do it in different words.

That's more or less what Dr Naston did:

Paragraph 1 + 2:	Motivating introduction, teamwork
Paragraph 3:	Comments on teamwork versus individualism
Paragraph 4:	Back to teamwork

Ⓢ Spice up your speeches

Figures of speech

Three forms of repetition

There are several forms of repetition to emphasise an idea.

1. Repetition of the same word within a sentence:
   The most important, my friends, *the most important* is teamwork.

2. Expressing one idea with two different words, the stronger of which is placed at the end:
   I assure you that initiative is *desired* and *needed* here.
   There is nothing so destructive to *motivation* and *enthusiasm.*

3. Repetition and variation of the key theme in the speech. Dr Naston has varied his key theme of co-operation like this:
   teamwork – the Ruver team – Ruver as a whole – like a good cricket team – work within the framework of the team

Emphasis with *do, does, did*

Another way of highlighting a verb is by using grammar and your voice. Instead of *we want to stimulate your motivation,* Dr Naston said this to stress his intention:
*We **do*** want to stimulate your motivation. (putting stress on *do)*

By the way, you can do this only in sentences without auxiliaries (Hilfsverben wie *be, have, will*). There are other grammatical ways of emphasising an idea which will be dealt with in later chapters.

How to discipline the audience

I don't mind people looking at their watches when I'm making a speech, but it is a damned nuisance to see them shaking them to see if they are still going.

Task 4: Highlight your verbs

Put stress on the verbs in italics – if possible – using a form of *do*.

1. Success *depends* primarily on co-operation.
2. The same *is* true for our company.
3. Each member of the team *has* his own job to do.
4. He *wanted* to stimulate your motivation.
5. You *may* be pleased to hear that the restaurant *will* be enlarged.

Task 5: Discover the spices

1. Dr Naston uses two metaphors to create a "we"-feeling.
2. He used an image drawn from the field of games to criticise individualism and selfishness.

Speaker's corner: A speaker's dilemma

The *purpose* of your speech is to inform, motivate or *convince* your audience. You want to *get a message across* to them, a message which they should not forget, a message that should change their *attitude* or *behaviour*, a message that should make them take action. But don't be too *confident*.

Zweck, Ziel
überzeugen; eine Botschaft vermitteln; Einstellung
Verhalten
zuversichtlich

This is what the biologist Konrad Lorenz (Nobel prize) has said about the speaker's dilemma:

When you tell them, they may not hear you.
They may hear you, but not listen to you.
They may listen, but not understand you.
If they understand, they may not *agree*.
If they agree, will they remember your message?
If they remember, they might not *take action*.
Even action may not change their behaviour.

zustimmen
handeln

Now that's where psychology and rhetoric come in.

Limitation — *Beschränkung*

If you want people to remember what you are going to say, don't tell them too much *at a time*. Limit your speech to two or three messages.

at a time — *auf einmal*

Appeal to emotions

If you want the audience to remember what you tell them, *appeal to* their emotions. Use figures of speech and *visual* language. If you want them to do what you ask, play the psychological card. Appeal to their basic needs.

appeal to — *ansprechen*
visual — *bildhaft*

1. Physical needs: they include the need of food, sex and *protection* from danger and harm.
2. Psychological needs like the need of love and *self-esteem*.
3. Social needs: status, *praise*, *belonging* and conformity.

protection — *Schutz*
self-esteem — *Selbstachtung*
praise, *belonging* — *Lob, Zugehörigkeit*

Repetition

Parents and teachers know that if they want to make people do something, they have to repeat things*: Muß ich euch alles dreimal sagen*? is one of the most *frequently* used sentences in the education of *mankind*.

frequently — *häufig*
mankind — *Menschheit*

And therefore I will repeat the **Three-T-Formula** again:

1. Tell them what you're going to tell them.
2. Tell them what you have to tell them.
3. Tell them what you have told them.

Chapter 7

Speaking to convince

In the engine development department at Ruver. K.H. Filsinger (**F**), Head of Engine Design, is talking to Dr Tisman (**T**), Head of Research, about a new diesel engine.

F: We have to adapt our major ranges to use diesel. The whole political thing has gone in that direction, for better or for worse.

T: We already have diesel in our off-road ranges and, of course, our jeeps and four-wheel drives.

F: I know that, but it has to be introduced everywhere. Also for normal family cars. Perhaps not in the sports range, but in all the rest.

T: I understand what you're saying. You'll have to present a strong case to the Board. Think of the cost involved.

How good a speaker are you?

Excellent:	You talk like a god.
Good:	You talk like an angel.
Average:	You talk to yourself.
Unsatisfactory:	You argue with yourself.
Hopeless:	You lose the argument.

(*) Diesel versus petrol (*)

Dr Koutert introduces the speaker and announces the theme.

Gentlemen, Mr Filsinger will now speak to you about developments for the next five years. Mr Filsinger, we're very interested to hear your point of view. The floor is yours.

Good evening, Gentlemen.
First, let me express my gratitude for the opportunity of being able to speak to you here this afternoon on the issue of future developments in engines. I'd like to come straight to the point. In motor magazines, in trade journals and in environmental publicity the question and the advantages of the diesel engine are being intensively discussed – and parallel to this, the anti-social reality of the petrol engine, that polluting monstrosity of the twentieth century, as some observers have described it. So, Gentlemen, in the media at present there is a trend towards the diesel motor and against petrol, and I would like to emphasise once more, we at Ruver have put our money on petrol.
Don't get me wrong, Gentlemen, petrol was the right decision five years ago. It is even now, though it should only be part of the solution. To be at the state of the art we need both directions – both technologies, Gentlemen, to support each other and to complement each other, and last but not least to play a vital role in reducing pollution and striding forwards into the future. To be a lasting part of all our futures.
Before you raise various arguments against this form of technology, please allow me to summarise for you the gist of the diesel's advantages. You all know that, in my capacity as an engineer, I have been closely involved in the design and development of petrol engines. How can I be against them? Quite the opposite, in fact. However, I can verify that the modern diesel engine emits far less pollution in its exhaust than its petrol-driven sister. Moreover, let me add, the particle size of diesel exhaust is becoming smaller and smaller. Testing standards are rising, and diesel technology is rising to the challenge. This is even recognised by the government. They've reduced taxes for diesel engines. What more proof do you require that diesel is the right way forward?

And what about the old question of performance? "Not as good as petrol, too slow, no acceleration etc." Well, Gentlemen, here are some facts! Diesel engines no longer sound like tractors, their acceleration depends on the weight and the model, but is not more than one second slower from zero to one hundred than the petrol motor. Exhaust-fume odour has been tested and found to be less than in its sister. And it can travel at the same cruising speed. Technologies have changed, become upgraded. Everybody, young and old, rich and poor, they can all successfully live with diesel. Gentlemen, I've taken enough of your time. Please listen to the words of an engineer, and of your marketing department. Let's stride into the future, diesel and petrol, hand in hand, motor for motor.

W Working with the language

Task 1: Key words in business

Can you fill in the missing words?

.... a range to use diesel	*eine Produktreihe auf Diesel umstellen*
.... a case to the Board	*ein Anliegen/Fall der Firmenleitung vortragen*
think of the cost	*an die entstehenden Kosten denken*
.... one's money ... petrol	*sein Geld auf Benzin setzen/in Benzin investieren*
.... and complement each other	*sich gegenseitig stützen und ergänzen*
.... pollution	*die Umweltverschmutzung verringern*
.... arguments against ...	*Argumente gegen ... anführen*
summarise the .... of the diesel's advantages	*die wichtigsten Vorteile von Dieselkraftstoff zusammenfassen*
be ... the state of the	*auf dem neuesten Stand der Technik sein*

be .... in the development of engines	*mit der Entwicklung von Motoren befaßt sein*
a question of	*eine Frage der Leistung*
technology has been	*die Technik ist verbessert worden*

Task 2: Thinker's corner

1. What is the effect of "*I'm not against them* (petrol engines). *Quite the opposite, in fact*"?
2. "*In motor magazines, in trade journals and in environmental publicity* the question and the advantages of the diesel engine is being intensively discussed." Why doesn't the speaker simply say *'in the press'*?
3. Why doesn't he just say *people* instead of "*young and old, husband and wife, rich and poor* ..."?

Task 3: Four ways of saying it

These linking words introduce a counter-argument. However, one would change the meaning? Tick it off.

However, I can verify that the modern diesel engine emits far less pollution in its exhaust than its petrol-driven sister.

- ☐ but
- ☐ yet
- ☐ and
- ☐ nevertheless
- ☐ on the other hand

Task 4: Three ways of saying 'thank you'

Fill in the missing letters.

1. I grat........ accept
2. I am deeply grat....... to you for
3. Let me express my grat....... for

} the opportunity of being able to speak to you here.

Task 5: Say it the speaker's way

What he meant …	and how he put it.
1. Let's hear what you have to say.	The ……. is ………
2. I won't waste your time.	I'd like to come …… to the …..
3. I have nothing more to say.	I've …… enough of your ……

Task 6: How to introduce a speaker

Replace *Wogglish* with English.

1. I have the great pleasure of *woggling* Mr X.
2. We have the honour of *woggling* addressed by Professor X on the theme of pollution.
3. Mr X, will now *woggle* to you about the problem of …
4. We're all *woggling* forward to your presentation.
5. Mr X, we're very *woggled* to hear your *woggle* of view.

✔ Checkpoint: Checklist for persuaders

1. Research how other people feel about your topic.
2. Select the most effective arguments.
3. Present your weak arguments first, your strong ones last.
4. Weaken the strongest counter-argument first, the weakest last.
5. Supply your arguments with good examples, facts and figures.
6. Take into account possible objections from the audience.
7. Restate your arguments at the end.
8. Paint the future bright.
9. Appeal for action.
10. Don't ever lose sight of what you want the audience to do.

Time for a smile

A young Conservative politician was being given a hard time at a rowdy public meeting. Exasperated by all the interruptions, he exclaimed, "I can hardly hear myself speak."
A voice from the crowd cried, "You're not missing much."

Ⓑ Building your speeches

The Five-Finger-Formula

The Five-Finger Formula can help you to write and memorise your speech. Move each finger when you come to the next part.

Thumb	1. Catch listeners' attention. 2. Tell them what you are going to talk about.
Forefinger	1. Describe the problem or the situation. 2. Give examples.
Middle finger	1. Weaken the counter-arguments, the strongest first, the weakest last. 2. Present your arguments or your solution. Weak arguments first, strong arguments last.
Ring finger	1. Show the advantages. 2. Present examples and supporting evidence.
Little finger	1. Summarise your arguments. 2. Ask them to take action. 3. Thank them for their attention.

Ⓢ Spice up your speeches

Figures of speech

Ellipsis

It is an incomplete sentence. One word or more have been left out, but the meaning can be understood without it/them. It reduces the sentence to a slogan or key phrase in order to draw the attention to the message.

Example: *To the cinema?* instead of *Are you going to the cinema?*

Personification

An object or an idea is treated as a human being. It illustrates your speech and gives a dramatic effect.

Example: Winter *spreads* its white sheet over hills and valleys.

Splitting up nouns

It is the opposite of generalising. It makes your speech less abstract and boring.

Example: Fun, fun, fun, for *mother, father* and *the little ones* (instead for *the whole family*).

Task 7: Discover the spices

Identify the figures of speech and say what Mr Filsinger wanted to achieve by using them.

1. Let's stride into the future, diesel and petrol, hand in hand, motor for motor.
2. To be at the state of the art we need both directions to support each other. To be a lasting part of all our futures.
3. Everybody, young and old, rich and poor, they can all successfully live with diesel.
4. I can verify that the modern diesel engine emits far less pollution in its exhaust than its petrol-driven sister.

Speaker's corner: Speaking to persuade

One of the most outstanding examples of a *contemporary* person who *has achieved success* because of his speaking *skills* is Lee Iacocca, the former CEO of the Chrysler Corporation. He used his talent as a speaker to win the *backing* of the President, Congress, and the American public in the largest *corporate bailout* in America's history. Even Iacocca credits his success to his skills as a speaker. In his autobiography, he writes: "I've seen a lot of guys who are smarter than I am and a lot who know more about cars. And yet I've left most of them in the smoke. Why? Because I'm tough? No. You've got to know how to talk to people, plain and simple." All *persuasive* speakers have these things in common:

1. They provide information so that the audience knows what to do.
2. They try to overcome the listeners' *objections*.
3. They appeal to emotions and *trust*.
4. They *move* the listener to action.

And while speaking they all know that their success depends only up to 10 maybe 20 per cent on what they have to say. The rest is voice and body language.
And they know that in this type of speech their argumentation has to be based on accurate logic. Nothing is more *destructive* than errors in logic. These are the biggest mistakes you should *avoid*:

Oversimplification
These are the alternatives – to limit our range to the petrol engine and stay *in the red* or to favour the diesel and *break even*.

zeitgenössisch
erfolgreich sein
Fähigkeiten
Unterstützung
Firmenrettung
überzeugend
Einwände
Vertrauen
bewegen, drängen
vernichtend
vermeiden
Vereinfachung
rote Zahlen schreiben; aus den roten Zahlen kommen

Begging the question

The question we have to answer is whether we should follow the advice of a young engineer and introduce the diesel. (No, the *issue* is whether to introduce the diesel.)

am Thema vorbeireden

Problem, Thema

Misleading statistics

Someone once said that there are "liars, damned liars and statistics". Even if your figures are true, some sharp fellow might find out that they do not prove what you *claim*.

behaupten

Obvious manipulation

Don't imitate those politicians: "We could create more jobs if we sent all the *foreigners* home."

Ausländer

Battle of words

We all know the *know-all* among the audience who is genetically programmed to ask the most *awkward* question, to sit with a *disapproving* look on his face, to *interrupt* or to undermine your efforts. If he tries to provoke you, stay calm. A good way of dealing with him is to ask him politely to repeat his question.

Besserwisser

unbequem; mißbilligend; unterbrechen

Don't *retaliate*, you might lose the battle of words. Only the best of speakers like Mrs Thatcher have the laugh on their side. She is said to have given a speech to a rather aggressive audience in a *rural* area. Suddenly a large *cabbage* was thrown at her. It just missed her ear but she didn't even *blink*. Her comment: "I suppose one of my opponents has lost his head."

zurückschlagen

ländlich; Kohlkopf

mit der Wimper zucken

Singing a person's praises

A telephone call between the Chairman of the Board, Dr Naston (**N**) and Dr Mayer (**M**), Member of the Board for Finance:

N: Hello, it's Naston here. There's a small matter I wanted to mention. It's about Koutert.

M: I can guess what you're going to say. An official word of congratulations on his promotion.

N: Yes, and if you don't mind, I'd prefer you to hold it on my behalf.

M: No problem, but I'm not particularly creative with these things, you know.

N: You don't need to be. Just list up your notes, what we should include etc and send them to PR, to Grosleger. He'll parcel it up for you.

Singing someone's praises

Okay, so he's young, but look at his experience.
Since he's been with the company, he's gone through sales,
marketing, planning, expansion, consolidation, reorganisation
and now ... puberty!

Replying to flattery

Thank you, Trevor, for those words of flattery. I think
I have some idea now, of how a pancake feels
when they pour syrup on it.

(*) For he's jolly good fellow (*)

At the meeting of the inner circle of the top management of Ruver at the Prince Charles Hotel in Warwick. Dr Mayer is speaking.

(*Fade in*) ... and that's everything on the question of customers' complaints today. Now to a more pleasant topic. First, let me tell you a little story about one of our colleagues. He joined us six years ago, at a time when things were not looking so good here at Ruver. I remember it well because I was involved. He was responsible for our smallest range which wasn't selling well at all, the Ruvlet 205. In my capacity as Financial Director I told him I was considering reducing the budget, or even eliminating it for this product. He absolutely didn't want to accept my decision and insisted I should give him a week to check it all out. Although he was new to the company he was able to grab the bull by the horns – no, not what you're thinking. He was successful in getting a small team of engineers together who were committed to completing the project by working indefinitely at weekends and the evening. "Let's go for it and you won't be sorry!" These were the words of Dr Koutert, Head of Research. Since then he has never looked back.

In that project he had more than two hundred percent success, a trend which has continued. And I believe his motivation, dedication and determination are a lesson for all of us. They are certainly contagious!

Dr Koutert is often strict, some would say too strict. However, this strictness is only a desire to design our products as optimally as possible. For the benefit of our commercial interests and out of loyalty to the principles of engineering! He is a gifted scientist and at the same time a creative manager of people who places a priority on teamwork and interpersonal skills. And all this to achieve the optimum from himself, from his team, for the benefit of the company.

In the last six years "Rowdy" Koutert, as he is fondly known in some circles, has been the new boy, a project leader, a department leader, head of research and finally a Member of the Board. But he still remains just as he was when he first joined us. Accessible, clear-minded and going down his line. You certainly know where you are with him, whether office worker or Board Member. He also keeps a firm hold on the grass

roots, the real work. Dr Koutert will wear his first hat as a director and manager, his second as an engineer amongst engineers.
Dr Koutert, we are happy to welcome you to the Board, a step which I am sure all executives present understand and will support. We wish you the best of luck with your two hats! Wear them honourably!

A clever reply

Thank you, Dr Mayer, for your kind words. It seems that I shall now have to say two prayers for forgiveness: the first for our Dr Mayer for telling so many lies in praising me; the second for myself – for enjoying it so much.

Working with the language

Task 1: Key words in business

.... something up	*etwas verpacken*
be .... for a product	*für eine Produktreihe verantwortlich sein*
.... reducing a budget	*erwägen, ein Budget zu kürzen*
a product .... well	*ein Produkt verkauft sich gut*
.... a budget for a range	*das Budget für eine Produktreihe streichen*
accept a	*eine Entscheidung akzeptieren*
.... oneself to completing a project	*sich der Vollendung eines Projekts verschreiben*
.... products optimally	*Produkte optimal entwickeln*
.... a .... on teamwork	*Teamwork Vorrang einräumen*
..... the .... of our commercial interests	*zum Wohl unserer geschäftlichen Interessen*
.... the .... from a team	*das Beste aus einem Team herausholen*

Task 2: Thinker's corner

1. What is the effect of the anecdote in the introduction?
2. What would you say is the main idea of this speech?
   A. to say thank you to Dr Koutert
   B. to emphasise teamwork
   C. to warn employees that Dr Koutert will be strict with them

Task 3: How many ways of saying it?

Which of the other five words doesn't show a contrast between **A** and **B**? Tick it off.

A: *Although* he was new to the company
B: he was able to grab the bull by the horns

- ☐ **1.** even if
- ☐ **2.** also
- ☐ **3.** in spite of the fact that
- ☐ **4.** nevertheless
- ☐ **5.** yet

(!) Beef up your word power

How to structure your speech

Beginning	Middle	End
First of all …	In the second place …	Finally …
In the first place …	The next point I want to make is …	Let me conclude by saying …
To begin with …	This brings me to my second point.	Well, that completes my end of things.

How to add a point

Moreover …	Besides …
Furthermore …	In addition to that …

Task 4: Wordbuilder's corner

1. Find the adjective to praise a business person with.

ability	....	*fähig*
commitment	....	*engagiert*
creativity	....	*schöpferisch*
dedication	....	*pflichtbewußt*
determination	....	*entschlossen*
discipline	....	*diszipliniert*
efficiency	....	*tüchtig*
honesty	....	*ehrlich*
ingenuity	....	*erfinderisch, genial*
loyalty	....	*treu*
reliability	....	*zuverlässig*
strictness	....	*streng*

2. What are business people if they …

have success	they are ....
have a clear mind	they are ....
work hard	they are ....
help others	they are ....
know a lot	they are ....

(B) Building your speeches: The Five-C-Formula

A safe approach to a speech for occasions like anniversaries, promotions or retirements is the Five-C-Formula. After greeting the audience you might go on like this:

1. Common experiences: Tell a story, an episode from the person's life you have in common and which is typical for him or her.
2. Characteristics: Pay tribute to achievements. Appreciate positive qualities. Mention nicknames or quotations if they explain the character.
3. Creating community spirit: If you are a people manager, you highlight those characteristics which you want the team or the staff to imitate or identify with.
4. Congratulations and best wishes for the future.
5. Cheers stands for a toast – if you can think of a suitable one.

The Toast

I drink to your health when I'm with you
I drink to your health when alone
I drink to your health so often
I'm becoming concerned at my own.

(S) Spice up your speeches

Figures of speech

Extended metaphor

You extend a metaphor when you widen its meaning or carry it on in the following sentences. The image becomes more complex and meaningful.

We wish you the best of luck *with your two hats*!
Wear them honourably!

Hyperbole

You create a hyperbole if you deliberately and obviously exaggerate an idea to produce an effect.

> The new Ruver Off-lander – the *greatest/most powerful temptation* since Adam and Eve.

Climax

It is a series of phrases arranged in order of increasing rhetoric effect.

> The new Ruver Mini is not only *inexpensive*,
> but also *comfortable* and *powerful*.

Task 5: Find the spices

Identify these figures.

1. And all this to achieve the optimum from himself, from his team, for the benefit of the company.
2. And I believe his motivation, dedication and determination are a lesson for all of us.
3. Mr Koutert has been the new boy, a project leader, a department leader, head of research and a Member of the Board.
4. In that project he had more than two hundred percent success, a trend which has continued.

Deadly Spices

1. Avoid clichés or stereotypes

A cliché is a phrase or an idea which is used so often that it is no longer interesting or effective.

> *He's worth his weight in gold; He's got a heart of gold; She is gentle as a lamb; He's a man of action.*

Some speakers use stereotypes to produce a humorous effect.

Although he was new to the company he was able *to grab the bull by the …* (no, not what you're thinking, but by the horns).

2. Beware of 'non-words'

Non-words are gap-fillers like *well, ok, etcetera, and so on, as you know, if you know what I mean …* . Non-words are barriers to clear communication. They show that you have not prepared your speech. Use a pause instead. Pauses are natural and can be very effective.

3. Don't generalise

As a speaker you must be credible if the audience is to trust you. Your credibility is at stake if you exaggerate or generalise.

Don't say:	**Say:**
all of our clients are …	most of our clients …
we *always* do …	we generally do
everybody knows that …	most people know that …

4. Eliminate qualifiers

Qualifiers are little words and phrases we use when we cannot think of the right word. If something is *more or less* unimportant, the audience might wonder 'Is it important or not?' Always call a spade a spade – to use a generalisation *and* a cliché.

Don't say:	**Say:**
we have *sort of a* problem	we have a delivery problem
it is *kind of a* household device	it is a vacuum cleaner

Speaker's corner: How to praise a person

A *eulogy* (laudatio) is a speech given in praise of a person at *funerals* and memorial services, but they can also be delivered at *retirement* parties or any occasion when someone is being honoured.

Lobrede
Begräbnis
Pensionierung

Collect information
Start with a story or an anecdote from the person's life. If you can't find any, look up the person's *curriculum vitae* or interview colleagues who know the person better than you.

Lebenslauf

Be *selective*
Limitation is the spice of speech. Focus on one or two of the subject' s positive qualities. *Wrap* them *up* in anecdotes from the person's life.

wählerisch
Beschränkung
verpacken

Adapt to the audience
Before you concentrate on a few specific qualities of the person being honoured, make sure that your audience will be able to identify with them. For example, a eulogy for a retiring manager might concentrate on a person's *helpfulness*, reliability, motivation and *ingenuity*. This approach will both honour the person and persuade the audience to follow his or her example. Words are what hold society together.

Hilfsbereitschaft
Erfindungsreichtum

Be *credible*
We are no *saints*, none of us are. Don't heap too much praise on the person. A eulogy for a *deceased* director might emphasise the person's high *standards* in order to honour the individual and to make people set *similar* high standards for themselves. But you may also include a touch of criticism – some minor, all too human *flaws of character* like impatience, strictness or *seriousness*.

glaubhaft
Heilige
verstorben
Leistungsnormen
ähnlich
Charakterfehler; Ernst

Chapter 9

The mission statement

Dr Koutert (**K**), Member of the Board, is discussing the mission statement of the Business Unit Off-Road Vehicles with Henry Smith (**S**), the Business Unit Leader.

K: So, now that we're going to have our Web-site on the Internet we have to have an overall mission statement.
S: That's a huge operation. What about the individual business units? How do they fit in?
K: That's the point. Each business unit will have its own Web-site, of course, all under one umbrella. So your task is to make a "speech" in the written form. And remember, it's for the Internet reader, so it's kiss, keep it simple, short!
S: What about sound and pictures to klick on?
K: Good idea. I suggest we get a professional actor to record the text.
S: And we need also a female voice to appeal to the more adventurous gentle sex as well, don't we?
K: Yes, and get one of our copy writers to handle the visuals.

Time for a smile

The newly appointed chairman of a group of companies was nervously studying the notes for his speech when the toastmaster walked up to him and asked, "Are you ready to speak, sir? Or shall we allow them to enjoy themselves a little longer?"

(*) A multi-media message on the Net (*)

Ruver Off-road Vehicles –
flexible technology to cope with the unknown! *(male voice)*

You want to get a snappy, clear image of who we are, of what we offer, of what we can achieve in partnership with our customers?
Let us introduce ourselves to you. Our name is Ruver Off-road Vehicles – called Ruvoff for short. A big name in the market for jeeps of all sorts and four-wheel drive cars in general. We are proud to be a leading player in this field. A little giant in a dynamic, off-road world!

What about our range? *(female voice)*

We don't have many cars in this off-road world, but what we do have are all winners. And they cover the needs of the driver who wants to measure himself against the environment. [Press this button for a video test with Mika Slippermaker in your favourite Ruver.]

The team consists of:
Land Ruver Overlander
Ranger and Jeeplet

Whatever range you choose, you will meet
power, reliability, and innovation.

What about ourselves and our goals? *(male voice)*

It is our ambition to offer our customers perfect products which they can trust and have confidence in. When we have made an agreement with our customer it is our objective to build a lasting relationship with him and to give sensible advice to the customer's benefit.
We will make it our business to listen to our customer's feedback and also to his requirements for the future. This will result in us both having the same objectives and allowing us to row in the same direction. [Press this button and learn why prominent customers like Boris Jezlin and Magaret Toucher drive an Overlander.]

Meet our Staff *(female voice)*

We are all part of a well-disciplined, well-trained and well-oiled machine. We are still perfecting our processes, which are in a state of permanent change adapting to customers' needs and the commercial environment. Further education and training is a keyword in our business unit. We work as individuals, but interact as part of a whole.

Our suppliers *(male voice)*

Our relationship to our suppliers is not bad at all. Nevertheless, it is our intention to further develop a lasting and mutually beneficial link with all our suppliers at home and abroad. This is the first link in the chain and plays a vital role. We aim to develop alongside those who produce our purchased parts, to raise quality and therefore to offer enhanced quality for our customers.
Suppliers, staff and customers – it is our aim to draw these three threads of business practice together into a powerful cord in which everyone can trust.

Your heart's content
is our intent
Ruver Off-Road Vehicles

Time for a smile
Lyndon B. Johnson on a speech by Richard Nixon:
I may not know much but I know chicken shit
from a chicken salad.

W Working with the language

Task 1: Key words in business

everything under one	*alles unter einem Dach*
be a .... player in a	*ein führender Mitspieler auf einem Gebiet sein*
.... the needs of the driver	*die Bedürfnisse des Fahrers abdecken*

build a lasting .... with the customer	*eine dauerhafte Beziehung zum Kunden aufbauen*
.... a beneficial link with the suppliers	*eine vorteilhafte Beziehung zum Lieferanten weiterentwickeln*
.... to customers' needs	*sich den Bedürfnissen der Kunden anpassen*
.... to .... the customers perfect products	*danach streben, den Kunden perfekte Produkte anzubieten*
offer .... quality for the customer	*dem Kunden verbesserte Qualität anbieten*
give .... to the customer's	*den Kunden zu seinem Vorteil beraten*
be in a .... of permanent	*sich in stetem Wandel befinden*
.... the business	*die Geschäftsabläufe perfektionieren*

Task 2: Thinker's corner

1. Why should this mission statement be short, dynamic and concise?
2. What effect does the repetition "well-disciplined, well-trained and well-oiled" achieve?
3. Is the overall direction of the statement general or specific in your opinion? Explain!

What to say to the audience

I think I should begin by explaining that on occasions like this, the length of the speech I make is proportional to the fee I'm paid; the higher the fee, the longer the speech.
So thank you all very much … good night.

Task 3: Five ways of saying it

How to say what you *want* without using *want*.
Use words for *Ehrgeiz, Ziel, streben* etc.

1. We *want* to develop alongside those who produce our parts to raise quality.
   We .... to develop alongside those who produce our parts, to raise quality.
2. *We have always wanted* to offer our customers perfect products.
   Our .... is to offer our customers perfect products.
3. *We want* to draw these three threads together into a powerful cord.
   Our .... is to draw these threads together into a powerful cord.
4. *We want* to further develop a link with all our suppliers.
   Our .... is to further develop a link with all our suppliers.
5. *We want you to be* content.
   Your heart's content is our ....

Task 4: Highlighting your ideas

Type 1: In chapter 6 you've already emphasised activities (verbs). Try it again with these sentences:

1. I *want* to stimulate your motivation.
2. We don't have many cars, but what we *have* are all winners.
3. And they *cover* the needs of the driver.

Type 2: You can also highlight a noun or a part of sentence by starting your sentence with *It is/was/has been.*

Highlight the words in *italics*

1. To offer our customers perfect products has always been our *ambition.*
2. *Our aim* is to draw these three threads of business practice together into a powerful cord.
3. *Our intention* is to further develop a link with all our suppliers.

(B) Building your mission statement on the Web-site

Something important is happening on the World Wide Web. It is welcoming hundreds of new businesses every week. For many growing companies, throwing up a Web-site in the middle of cyberspace may be the right choice. Establishing a Web-site is like setting up shop downtown on a crowded city street.

You're accessible to perhaps millions of people. And you've got complete control over what your store looks like. Any Internet user with Web browser software and your Web address can zip straight to your 'store' and check out what you offer. Not only can visitors read your message, they can also listen to it and click on your showroom to see your products on video or slides.

Your mission statement could be part of your site.

1. Introduce the company
2. Present your product range
3. Present the staff
4. Give testimonials from customers
5. Name your suppliers
6. Draw it all together.

How to involve the audience

The entire American sales force of Frisky Dog Food was gathered together for their national sales convention. In the auditorium the marketing director was using the old pattern of call and response to work up the spirits of his team.

"Who's got the greatest dog food in North America?"

"We have!"

"And who's got the greatest advertising campaign?"

"We have!"

"Who's got the most attractive packages?"

"We have!"

"Who's got the biggest distribution?"

"WE HAVE!"

"Okay. So why aren't we selling more of the product?"

One bold voice from the crowd replied,

"Because the damned dogs don't like it."

Ⓢ Spice up your speeches

Figures of speech

Slogans

A slogan is a phrase that is easy to remember, used by a political party or in advertising to attract people's attention or to suggest an idea quickly.
Power to the people.

Litotes

You highlight an idea effectively if you use the opposite in negative form. It is often used to add a pinch of irony to your sentence or to create a humorous effect.
Instead of saying *Mr Dobson is very lazy*, you might say:
Mr Dobson is *not exactly one of our most hardworking employees.*

Trias

Psychologists have found out that a sequence of three ideas is more easily remembered than separate ones, in different sentences. This is how a German company advertises its chocolate bars:
Square, handy, good.
The program of the French Revolution was: *Liberté, Egalité, Fraternité.*

Task 5: Say it the speaker's way

Reformulate these sentences using the litotes.

1. We *have few* cars in this off-road world, but what we do have are all winners.
2. We *have quite a good* relationship to our suppliers.
3. We are a *relatively small* company.

How to criticise a speaker

A guy with your IQ
should have a low voice too!

Task 6: Find the spices

Identify the figures of speech.

1. .... Whatever range you choose, you will meet power, reliability, and innovation.
2. .... Suppliers, staff and customers – it is our aim to
3. .... draw these three threads of business practice together into a powerful cord in which everyone can trust.

Speaker's corner: Your voice as your medium

Why does Dr Koutert suggest hiring professional actors to record the mission statement? He has read that your voice, tone, intonation, resonance, pauses and speed *account for* 84 per cent of the *credibility* you have when people can't see you. This is the case when you talk on the telephone or record a text for a slide show or a multimedia Web-site. Here is some *advice* for the rest of us who are no actors.

ausmachen
Glaubwürdigkeit
Rat

How to deliver the speech

Your voice is the primary vehicle to carry your message. It is like transport – you can have an old car that rattles along or a *smooth* running car. Both will get you to your *destination*, but the quality of the ride can vary greatly. The worst thing you can do is read your speech. Use notes and *outlines* of main ideas when you speak. This will allow you to let your mind select words spontaneously and force your voice to be active, *animated* and natural because you are continuously thinking, adapting, and altering your *content*.

ruhig, sanft
Ziel
Gliederung
lebhaft
Inhalt

How fast should you speak?
You should be speaking at about 120 to 150 words per minute. Find out by timing yourself. However, this *rate* is not uniform like the tick-tock of a clock. Good speakers present main ideas and difficult points at a slower *pace* than they do a joke. Follow these *rules of thumb*:

Geschwindigkeit
Geschwindigkeit
Daumenregel

Idea	Rate of Speech
complex	more slowly
serious	more slowly
humorous	more quickly
exciting	more quickly

***Emphasise* the right word**
Take the sentence "We will make it our business to listen to our customer's feedback". Read it, *emphasising* a different word each time. Notice the difference in the meaning, *depending on* which word you emphasise. Experiment, emphasising the right word in your everyday conversations.

betonen
betonen
abhängig von

Pause for effect
You can pause naturally for three to four seconds, even in the middle of a sentence. The problem is we are not *used to* doing it. When we do it, a three or four-second pause seems like 20 seconds in our own minds. Practise pausing and getting feedback to learn how you sound when you pause.

gewöhnt zu

How to practise
The best exercise for developing your vocal skills is to *record* yourself. Do it as often as possible. Record a telephone conversation, a business meeting, a conversation with a friend, etc. Even record *casual* conversations using a dictaphone. The most important way for your to *improve* your voice is to get audio feedback.

aufnehmen
lässig
verbessern

Chapter 10

Toast to the staff

Georg Grosleger receives an e-mail from Dr Koutert, Head of Research.

Dear Mr Grosleger,

On Friday 23, next week I am visiting the staff of my former business unit of Research & Development. I want to thank the men for the last six years of support and to give them a push forward to even greater things. The speech shouldn't be arrogant in any way. I'm certain you know what to emphasise on an occasion like this and I have full confidence in your eloquence. Above all the toast should be light and short, approximately two hundred words.

Time for a smile

The chairman of the board had to make an important speech at a meeting of the shareholders, and as usual he delegated the job of writing the speech to his personal assistant.
"Miss Smith, just put something together for me, will you? You know all the facts and figures. And make it short and sweet – about twenty minutes should do."
When he returned to the office after the meeting, he was in a furious temper. "What's the idea of writing me a one-hour speech?" he thundered. "Half of the audience walked out before I'd finished."
"With respect, sir, I wrote you a twenty-minute speech as you told me," replied the personal assistant. "However, you asked me to make two extra copies."

(*) Teamwork and loyalty (*)

Ladies and Gentlemen,
It is my privilege and pleasure to propose the health of the staff of R&D. The reason why it is a pleasure is that I welcome the opportunity to say a few things that I think every day. Whether work is a positive source of enjoyment, or merely a necessary evil, is a matter of opinion – personally I think it is a mixture of both; but there can be no doubt that it is a good deal more pleasant – or, if you like, a good deal less unpleasant – if it is done in a spirit of mutual co-operation. We have that spirit here to a very high degree. I hope we shall always keep it.
Now I am not going to make a high-flying speech about working for the honour and glory of the company. This is a business house, and we are in business to make money; and you work in the company with the same basic objective. But, as you have shown, there is no reason why even the "dirty" job of making money should not be made pleasant; and the way to make it pleasant is to work as a team. Teamwork means loyalty, and I know that no staff could be more loyal. I want you to know that your loyalty is appreciated.
I have talked enough. Ladies and Gentlemen, I propose the health of the staff, I couple with this toast the name of our old friend – old in service, but young in spirit – Mr Patten.

(B) Building your toast

Let's prepare the outline of a toast. Let's take a wedding as an example.

The opening

1. The first sentence is easy: "I have been asked to propose the health of .... Nothing gives me greater pleasure". Anyone can get that far!
2. Compliment entry: Say how honoured you are to be asked to speak. Pay compliments to whoever should be thanked among the audience.

The middle

1. What is to go in the middle? Think first about what you are trying to achieve. Choose one or two themes. Talk about the atmosphere and the working climate, the good business relationship with the business partner.
2. You then throw in a suitable quotation or some humorous advice for a happy retirement.

The closing

One good thing about a toast is that you don't have to worry about how to end the speech. You simply invite the audience to drink with you, and your closing words are a variation of "Please raise your glasses to our guests of honour."

Task 1: Thinker's corner

1. Can you give an example of irony in the speech?
2. How is Mr Patten complimented in the last paragraph of this toast?
3. What is the main purpose of Dr Koutert's speech to his staff?

Time for a smile

A speaker had just finished what he thought was one of his best after-dinner speeches. When he had finished, a drunk went over to him and said, "That was the most boring speech I have ever heard in my life."

The chairman who hadn't heard what he had said dragged the speaker away and said, "Sorry about old Tomkins. But pay no attention to what he says. When he's drunk he only repeats what everybody else is saying."

(*) A reply from the staff to the directors (*)

After a toast intended to motivate the staff, it is normal practice for one of those employees present to say a short word of thanks. It should closely reflect some of the comments made in the toast to the staff. Chief engineer in R&D, Tom Disney, is chosen to do it. Notice how he refers to ideas mentioned by Dr Koutert.

Ladies and Gentlemen,
Thank you for this unexpected honour of having to propose a spontaneous toast. Normally, I'm not a good speaker, so I have to prepare carefully in advance. This isn't possible this time as I couldn't know what Dr Koutert would say to us. Okay, that was the excuse for what is to follow. Please bear with me.
Well, first of all I'd like to say that on behalf of the staff I am happy to reply to this kind toast. It is easy for me to be sincere in my reply, for I have worked here happily for many years. I think my colleagues, old and young, share my happiness; and the fact that we are all so difficult to get rid of explains more than words what we feel about the company. I do not want to get sentimental, because it would be untrue if I were to suggest that the company takes up the whole, or even the major part, of our lives. Like many others here tonight, I am a family man, and my greatest joy is in my home. But there is here, too, something of a family spirit – a different sort of family, of course, as it must be; but it exists, and the place would be the poorer without it.
Like everyone else here tonight, I come to work in order to earn my living. But it has always been my simple philosophy that the mere fact that you do something because you have to is no reason for not liking to do it. Ladies and Gentlemen, I admit to you that I like my work; or rather, it is not so much my work that I like as the atmosphere in which I do it. I think that everyone contributes to that atmosphere; but it would be most unfair of me if I did not say that it could not exist without the active encouragement and participation of the directors and especially the rowdy one, whom we have all come to respect. If they have a loyal and co-operative staff, it is what they deserve. On behalf of the staff I thank you.

Task 2: Thinker's corner

1. Why does Tom Disney begin with his excuses in the first paragraph?
2. In the second paragraph there is a joke. Explain.
3. What is the main image in the speech?

Working with the language

Key words in 'toasting'

1. Toasting persons

It is my privilege and pleasure to propose the health of	*Es ist mir eine Ehre und ein Vergnügen, auf das Wohl von ... anzustoßen.*
I have been asked to propose the health of .... Nothing gives me greater pleasure.	*Ich bin gebeten worden, mit Ihnen auf das Wohl von ... zu trinken. Ich tue das mit dem größten Vergnügen.*
I'd like to make a toast to our new colleague.	*Ich möchte einen Toast auf unseren neuen Kollegen ausbringen.*
I rise to toast our guests.	*Ich erhebe mich, um auf das Wohl unserer Gäste zu trinken.*

2. Drinking to business situations

I'd like to propose a toast to the conclusion of our contract.	*Ich schlage vor, wir stoßen auf den Abschluß unseres Vertrags an.*
Let's raise our glasses to the future of the company.	*Erheben wir unsere Gläser und trinken auf die Zukunft der Firma.*
Let's celebrate our success with a glass of champagne.	*Begießen wir unseren Erfolg mit einem Glas Champagner.*

What to say to the audience

I'm delighted to see that you all have managed to come to this evening; you obviously didn't know that I was going to be making a speech.

3. Expressing wishes

Sincerest wishes for …	*Unsere aufrichtigsten Wünsche für …*
Take our best wishes with you.	*Nehmen Sie unsere besten Wünsche mit auf den Weg.*
I want to wish the newly wed couple all the best.	*Ich wünsche dem neuvermählten Paar alles Gute.*

4. Closing the toast

Here's to the company.	*Auf das Wohl der Firma.*
To your good health!	*Auf Ihr Wohl!*
Cheers!	*Prost!*

Task 3: Three ways of saying it

Can you complete the verbs?

make h . . . d	} a speech	make p . . . . . . s	} a toast

(S) Spice up your speeches

Not so serious toasts

Let us toast the fools.
But for them, the rest of us could not succeed. *Mark Twain*

To best friends who know the worst about us
but refuse to believe it.

Here's to us that are here
To you that are there
And the rest of everyone everywhere. *Rudyard Kipling*

To our wives and sweethearts. May they never meet.

Here's hoping you live forever …
And that mine is the last voice you hear.

Speaker's corner: All you ever wanted to know about toasts

The term toast *dates back* to the 1600s and refers to a *chunk* of bread dipped in drinks. The term then came to refer to a drink in honour of a favourite lady and soon, a drink in honour of just about anything sharp and witty.

A light-hearted toast is *required* for a great number of informal occasions including retirement, *farewell* and promotion celebrations and most

zurückgehen auf
Stück
benötigen
Abschied

business and office-orientated functions. If you're asked to propose a toast, try to keep it *brief* – two minutes is about the right length. You rarely hear *complaints* about a speech being too short, but you hear many people complain that a speech was too long.
Today, a toast is expected to *set the tone* for the entire event. For this reason, long jokes and stories are not in order, but brief jokes and amusing quotations are. You'll find plenty of them in this book. As with all other speeches, *ensure* that everything you have to say is entirely relevant and amusing and leads up to your main function – which is *encouraging* others to join you in a toast of good health or happiness.

kurz
Beschwerden
Stimmung machen
sicher gehen
ermutigen

How not to thank the host

First, let me thank our host for that wonderful introduction. It had all the sincerity of a Hollywood star crying "ouch" on her seventh honeymoon! ... Just kidding.

Chapter 11

Awarding an award

It's the custom in Battlemoore to choose the businessman or woman of the year. This year Battlemoore Chamber of Commerce has invited Ruver to sponsor the award. The young but promising trainee Tom Reckless (**R**) has been attributed the responsible task of delivering the speech. Tom is being briefed by Georg Grosleger (**G**) . Let's listen in.

R: Well, I'm afraid I've never done a job like that.

G: Never mind. Here's a foolproof checklist for this type of speech.

R: Why choose me? Wouldn't it ...?

G: As you know all our directors are at a congress on the Fiji Islands.

R: What about you? Wouldn't it be better if you went to Ballermoore instead of me.

G: Battlemoore, Battlemoore, don't forget! Well, I had thought of it, but some journalists are testing our Jeeplet tomorrow. You know, it's not foolproof yet, and I have to feed them the right information.

R: The right information! What about me? I've never heard of Battlemoore.

G: The local Chamber of Commerce will provide you with everything you need. All I know is that the award consists of a little trophy donated by Battlemoore Potteries and the proud sum of £500.

R: I'm a bit worried that ...

G: Nothing to be worried about. Stage fright – quite normal. You know where that place is? No? Here's a road map of the UK. Good luck.

Time for a smile

France: Jean Dupont, salesman of the year,
sold the Venus de Milo a spray deodorant.

(*) The 'Business woman of the year' award (*)

The 'Business woman of the year' award in the Town Hall of Battlemoore. Tom Reckless moves slowly over to the rostrum.

Ladies and Gentlemen,
Thank you all for coming here this evening to witness the presentation of the *Roosting Award* for the best young businessman or woman of the year. Ruver Offroad Cars is honoured to sponsor this year's event. As you may know, this impressive trophy, produced and donated by the local Battlemoore Potteries, is awarded each year to the most promising talent under the age of 30 in this lovely town. All the candidates have been noted for their outstanding results in the fields of business or science. And they had to undergo a gruelling examination of their business knowledge and acumen by your distinguished panel of judges. I extend a hearty thank-you to Mrs Busybody, Lord Picklewig and the director of the Chamber of Commerce, Mr Moose, who had the delicate task of nominating a winner among seven equally recommended competitors.
Last year's recipient of the Roosting Award, I'm pleased to be able to tell you, has already gone on to great things, helped, no doubt, by the reputation of the Roosting Award and the prize of £500 which accompanies it.
This year's worthy winner is Annette Sauter – and I doubt whether that news will surprise anyone who knows her. Annette's career as founder of IBM, Instant Baking Machines, has been quite meteoric. At the age of 12 she was already experimenting with new ways of bread-making in her uncle's bakery in Boarsbrook. Two years later, she had modified the central oven into what became known in her village as the FBA, the Fast Bread Automate. However, success didn't come easy to Annette. Even after a series of setbacks which forced her uncle to abandon the family enterprise, this young lady followed her dream and created ABB, the first automated bread baker for the housewife which – so I was told – is on show in Battlemoore Museum.
She has merited the award for both a new ingenious technical breakthrough and for her contribution to the welfare of your community.

Annette Sauter has further developed her FBA-99 into a small and light multi-purpose baking device which can process not only bread but also Battlemoore's fine pottery, for which your town is well-known far beyond the boundaries of this county.
I am very pleased, Annette Sauter, to be able to present you with this beautiful trophy and the title Battlemoore's Young Businesswoman of the Year – and, of course, this cheque for £500.

✔ Checkpoint: Awarding an award

Georg's checklist for award ceremonies

1. **Describe the award:** Give full details about the origin and the history of the award. Remember that there may be people present who know nothing whatsoever about the background of the event, so be as informative as possible.
2. **Name the sponsors:** Explain who they are, welcome them and thank them.
3. **Explain the procedure:** How are the candidates nominated? How are they selected? Who are the judges? Welcome the panel of judges if they are present and thank them for their trouble.
4. **Name the recipient:** Tell the audience who she or he is and what he or she has done to merit the award. A little anecdote would be in order at this stage.
5. **Present the award:** Ask the winner to step forward. Congratulate him and hand over the award. Ask for applause.
6. **Be modest:** Don't try to steal the limelight from the person being honoured. No rhetorical fireworks and figures of speech!

Time for a smile

It is said that the first speech given by Christopher Columbus after the meal which celebrated his discovery of the New World began: "A funny thing happened to me on the way to India."

Herbert v. Prochnow

Working with the language

Task 1: Key words in business

Find the verbs used in the speech.

.... a presentation	*attend* a presentation
.... an event.	*promote* an event
.... *a trophy*	*offer* a trophy
.... a prize ot the winner	*give* a prize to the winner
.... an examination	*sit for* an examination
be .... for one's results	be *distinguished* for one's results
.... a hearty thank-you to somebody	*say* a hearty thank-you to somebody
.... the family enterprise	*give up* the family enterprise

Task 2: Let's go woggling again

Do you remember the *woggles*? And can you replace them?

Annette has *woggled* the award for both a new ingenious technical *woggle*-through and for her *woggle* to the welfare of your community. Annette Sauter has further de*woggled* her FBA-99 into a small and light multi-*woggle* baking *woggle* which can *woggle* not only bread but also Battlemoore's fine pottery, for which your town is well-*woggled* far beyond the boundaries of this county.

The difference between a diplomat and a lady

When a diplomat says 'yes', he means 'perhaps'.
When he says 'perhaps', he means 'no'.
When he says 'no', he's no diplomat.

When a lady says 'no', she means 'perhaps'.
When she says 'perhaps', she means 'yes'.
But when she says 'yes', she's no lady.

✔ Checkpoint: The vote of thanks

If you ever find yourself in the pleasant position of receiving such an award, this is the pattern which your answer should follow.

1. **Don't prepare your speech:** A vote of thanks needs a spontaneous response to what has just been said, and by definition it can't be prepared in advance.
2. **Listen carefully:** Pay attention to what the speaker has to say and jot down the things you particularly want to comment on, and add any amusing lines or quotations you can think of.
3. **Express your gratitude:** Thank the panel of judges and the person making the award and the organisation he or she represents.
4. **Be brief:** A vote of thanks should take five minutes at the most; any longer and you'll be rivalling the guest speaker's contribution to the evening. Say what the award means to you.
5. **Outlook to the future:** Give a few hints about what you intend to do with the award and what your future plans are.

Annette's vote of thanks – her first draft

Ladies and Gentlemen, Dear Mr Reckless,
First of all I'd like to take the opportunity of thanking you for being with me tonight on the occasion of receiving this wonderful award. It's not very often that we hear much about small business succeeding. It's often a lot of work for little return. Well, in my case I was lucky and we've achieved two hundred per cent more turnover than we expected. I hope we can be an example for other young entrepreneurs. I am very pleased and grateful to accept this award for the most promising small business and, of course, the cheque for £500. Thank-you!

But Annette didn' like it. It was not personal enough. So she wrote a second speech, and you are invited to help her with it.

Task 3: Annette Sauter's vote of thanks

Fill in the words where they belong.
Change the form of the words if necessary.

keep	*sponsor*
choose	*imitate*
provide	*inspire*
regard	*open*
proud	*previous*
create	*panel*
express	*wealth*

I should like to .... my thanks to the .... of judges, to the Battlemoore Chamber of Commerce which has .... the award and in particular to you, Mr Reckless, for your kind words and to your company who .... so generously .... this event.
I'm very honoured and .... to have been .... to receive the Roosting Award, which is one of the most highly .... awards made in our part of the world. I .... the trophy on my desk at IBM, where I hope it will .... me to .... the success of .... winners. Expansion plans for IBM are already under way, and I hope to be .... a second small factory near Battlemoore in the next few months, ... more jobs and .... for this beloved town.

Food for thought

I fear I cannot make an amusing speech. I've just been reading a book which says that all geniuses are devoid of humour.
Stephen Spender

Once you've overcome your fear of public speaking, you'll never be asked to speak again.
Al Batt

Speaker's corner: Overcome your nervousness

"Stage fright – quite normal", said George to Tom Reckless. They all have stage fright, even politicians and actors. For all but the most extrovert, an invitation to make a speech is something to be *dreaded*. But it needn't be, particularly if you are in business. As a businessman you have some *advantages* when it comes to making public speeches.

Lampenfieber

fürchten

Vorteile

- If you are used to making presentations you won't have difficulties making a speech.
- As a business person you have a lot to talk about. Who doesn't have a funny story to tell about their *subordinates*, colleagues or bosses? And who hasn't experienced the pleasures and problems of office life?
- When you stand up to give a speech about the world of business, you can be sure that most of the people in your audience will be able to identify with you.
- As a businessman you are versed in the *art of persuasion*; you know how to *assess* customers, weigh up situations and respond appropriately. All these skills are directly *applicable* when it comes to making a public speech.

Untergebene

Überredungskunst

einschätzen

anwendbar

Advice from the experts

- You are the boss, the specialist. That is why you have been asked to hold the speech.
- Your audience comes to listen to you – and not to *evaluate* or criticise you. They are on your side.

beurteilen

- Only you and nobody else will notice if you do not follow your *outline* or forget an argument. Nothing to be nervous about!
- Get to know your audience *in advance*. Ask the host who is organising the *event*.
- Arrive well prepared with a clear outline of the speech. This gives you *security*.

Gliederung
im voraus
Ereignis
Sicherheit

- Arrive half an hour earlier to check the microphone and the visual media you will use.
- Get a glass of water. When you are nervous your mouth will be dry.
- Use anecdotes or *witty* quotations to break the ice. *geistreich*
- Don't be afraid of pauses. Take them when you need them. They don't *influence* your message. *beeinflussen*
- Take your time! *Breathe* deeply and don't talk too fast. The bigger the audience the more slowly you may speak. *atmen*
- Alcohol often *increases* nervousness. *verstärken*
- Some speakers overcome their stage fright by imagining their audience in silly situations, as pupils in a school. Winston Churchill liked to imagine them completely *naked*. *nackt*

Time for a smile

A bishop was presenting the awards at a school. He got tired of saying the same words of congratulations to each recipient. So, when a pretty blond girl came up to receive her prize he thought he would try something different.
"What are you going to do when you leave school, my dear?" he asked.
"Well bishop," she replied, "I was going home for tea. But I could cancel that."

Chapter 12

Speech to a retiring colleague

Dr Naston's secretary, Susan (**S**), telephones Georg (**G**)

S: Hi, Georg, how's it going?
G: Okay, I guess. I'm a bit depressed, though. Somehow I'm not on top of things at the moment.
S: That's normal on a Monday morning. Never mind, chin up. Listen, you know Dr Stow, don't you? He's retiring. If I give you the details, can you put together a speech? You know, let out all the stops.
G: I'll do my best.

Some niceties to build into a farewell speech

To a director:

On behalf of the Board I was asked to wish you all the best for your early retirement – it was a majority decision of five to four.

To your secretary:

Retirement is the time of life when you can stop lying about your age and start lying about the company.

(*) It is with a sense of real loss that we see him go (*)

Dr Stow, Head of the Patent Department is sixty-four years old and is taking early retirement. His boss and Member of the Board, Dr Naston, who has known him for more than a quarter of a century, makes a speech on his retirement.

Ladies and Gentlemen, Dear Tom,
On an occasion such as this our feelings are bound to be mixed. Dr Stow is leaving us today, after thirty years' continuous service with the company, to enjoy a well-deserved retirement. He takes with him our earnest wishes for his continued health and happiness for many years to come. Everybody would wish Dr Stow the rest he has earned after his years of hard work; yet we cannot pretend that we are happy to see him leave us. I do not want to say much about his value to the company, because that is a matter of which we shall be reminded for a long time to come. No one is indispensable, but there are some people it is very difficult to do without, as I fear we are shortly going to discover. We are going to miss our patent boss – but much more are we going to miss a man who has brought much humanity with him.
As is natural in an organisation of this kind, our respective relationships with Dr Stow have varied a good deal. To some he has been one of the bosses, to be called "Sir". Others have known him just as "Dr Stow". To others again, he has been simply "Stow"; and to a few intimate colleagues he has been plain "Tom". But his attitude to us has never reflected these differences. He has treated us all with the same courtesy and good humour. He has never been one to smile at the directors and scowl at the junior clerks – indeed, from my personal experience he has inclined rather to smiling at the juniors and scowling at the directors! By his cheerfulness and natural friendliness Dr Stow has earned the respect of every one of us, and it is with a sense of real loss that we see him go.
On behalf of the staff, I have the great pleasure of presenting Dr Stow with this small token of our esteem and affection. This is a farewell gift, but I know he will come to see us at times as a friend – if only to call by and smile at both juniors and directors – Dr Stow.

Working with the language

Task 1: Keywords in business

Do you remember these phrases?

.... early	*vorzeitig in Pension gehen*
a .... – .... retirement	*ein wohlverdienter Ruhestand*
.... after thirty years' continuous	*sich nach dreißigjähriger ununterbrochener Arbeit zurückziehen*
no one is	*niemand ist unentbehrlich*
it is difficult to .... him	*es ist schwer ohne ihn auszukommen*
.... the junior	*die Büroangestellten finster anblicken*
.... everybody with	*jedermann höflich behandeln*

Task 2: Thinker's corner

1. How often does Dr Naston mention that they will miss Tom Stow?
2. Which of Dr. Stow's qualities does Dr Naston mention?
3. Where is repetition used to stress Dr Stow's many sides?
4. Some listeners might get the impression that Dr Stow has not been one of the most valuable members of the staff. Why?

Time for a smile

I asked the chairperson for details of the people to whom I would be speaking today. "Could you please give the number of those present, broken down by age and sex?"
He replied, "Yes they are."
Clement Freud

Famous first words

Before I get to the work at hand, let me say that to be chosen as speaker for this occasion is ... more than an honour. We had to draw lots to see who would be the guest speaker. – I lost.

Task 3: Dropping themes

Sometimes speakers just mention a theme without going into details. They do this to show that they haven't forgotten it. Here are some more. Can you unscramble them? The first one has been done for you.

about/much/do/I/not/want/say/to/ Dr Stow's value to the company.
I do not want to say much about Dr Stow's value to the company.

1. I/going/not/upon/am/touch/to
2. I/want/not/to/bore/do/you/about/details/with
3. not/so/is/it/important/mention/to
4. I/waste/not/will/your/with/time
5. to/deal/I/going/am/with/not

} the numerous patents he filed for the company.

Task 4: Guided translation

How to express one's best wishes for a person.

1. (*Unsere aufrichtigen*) wishes for your (*Glück und Gesundheit)* accompany you.
2. I'm sure (*ich spreche für uns alle*) when I wish you a (*angenehmen*) and satisfying eve of life.
3. From the bottom of our (*Herzen*) we'd like to wish you (*das Allerbeste*) for the next (*Abschnitt*) in your life.
4. You know you take our (*besten Wünsche*) for a happy and (*erfolgreiche Zukunft)* with you.

What not to say to a retiring colleague

When he was a kid, like other youngsters he used to play 'Hide and Seek'. The trouble was, when he was hiding nobody noticed the difference.

Some people bring happiness wherever they go. Pete Bistro brings happiness whenever he goes.

Checkpoint: The Six-W-Formula

This formula helps you to prepare your speech.
It should include at least the main points 1, 2, 5, and 6.

1. **Who?** Greetings.
   Who is present? Greet them, don't forget the guest of honour, in our case Tom Stow.

2. **Why?** Introduction 1.
   Why is he or she leaving? Are they taking retirement, promoted to a different department, transferred to Headquarters etc.?

3. **Where?** Introduction 2.
   Where did you meet the person first (anecdote)? Where is he or she going?

4. **When?** A nostalgic look back in time.
   When did you first meet? How long have you been working together?

5. **What?**
   A. Character: What kind of person is he or she? What are their positive (negative) qualities?
   B. Success: What to thank the person for? What have his or her achievements or contributions to the company been?
   C. Defeats: What has he or she not achieved?
   D. Feelings: What does his or her departure mean to you?

6. **Wishes**: Closing.
   Express your best wishes for the future.
   Express your wish to keep in touch.
   Present the farewell present.

Be generous in praise. At the same time praise must not be overdone. If it is too much, the praise will lose its value.

(B) Building your farewell speech

Here is a general outline of a farewell speech.

A. Greet those present, address the guest of honour personally, say why you have come together.

B. Talk about one common experience or one memorable event which best reflects the person's value for the company and one or two qualities of character. Be selective!

C. Thank the person for his or her achievements and express your feelings of loss. Close with your best wishes for the future.

Golden rules to better English

1. Never use a long word where a short one will do.
   No: I'm afraid your clothes *are inappropriate to* the occasion.
   Yes: I'm afraid your clothes *do not suit* the occasion.
2. Never use the passive where you can use the active.
   No: These cars *are sold* like hot cakes.
   Yes: These cars *sell* like hot cakes.
3. Never use a scientific word or a jargon word if you can think of an everyday English equivalent.
   No: We offer all sorts of *domestic appliances.*
   Yes: We offer all sorts of *household machines.*
4. When in doubt – leave out.
   No: I'm afraid we *have got* a sort of a problem here.
   Yes: I'm afraid we *have* a problem here.
5. Break any of these rules rather than saying nothing, because communication in business is as important as style.

Food for thought

Retirement means twice as much husband
on half as much money.

Ⓢ Spice up your speeches

Variations on a theme

Did you notice that Dr Naston didn't have much to say about Dr Stow? That is why he repeated one theme not just three times but five times: his farewell feelings. However, he was careful to change the wording.

Task 5: Do you remember Dr Naston's feelings?

Fill in the missing letters.

1. It is with a _en_e of real lo__ that we see him go.
2. We shall be r_m__d_d of him for a long time to _om_.
3. We cannot p_e_end that we are happy to see him _ea_e us.
4. On an o__a_ion such as this our feelings are b__nd to be m__ed.
5. We going to m___ a man who has brought much _u_a_i_y with him.

Quotations, proverbs and clichés

Here are a few phrases to spice up a farewell speech

Einen Baum erkennt man an seinen Früchten.	The tree is known by its fruit.
Ein guter Mann ist schwer zu finden.	A good man is hard to come by.
Gute Leute sind selten.	Good men are scarce.
Tugend ist ihr eigener Lohn.	Virtue is its own reward.
Auch jene dienen, die nur stehen und warten.	They also serve who only stand and wait. (John Milton)
Abschied nehmen bedeutet immer ein wenig sterben.	Parting is such sweet sorrow.
Man muß manchmal von einem Menschen fortgehen, um ihn zu finden. (H. Doderer)	Sometimes you need to move apart to come together again.

Speaker's corner: Speaking with your arms and hands

Are you one of those speakers who do not know what to do with their hands when facing an unknown audience? Some *clench* their manuscripts, some *cling* to the *rostrum*, others cross their arms over their *chests*, again others let them *dangle* down or put one hand in their pocket and *fiddle* with their keys. Don't *imitate* that!

Experienced speakers use their hands to stress the meaning of their words by cutting the air with the *edge of their palm*, they raise a finger to call for attention or *reject* arguments by slightly pushing the air towards the audience.

Your arm has got four parts: hand, *forearm*, upper arm plus shoulder. You can move them together or individually. It *depends* on how many people you have sitting in front of you.

umklammern
festhalten; Rednerpult; Brust
hängen
spielen; nachahmen
Handkante
zurückweisen
Unterarm
abhängen

What to do

- Small *gestures*: If you speak to a group of three or four, just use your fingers and the *palm* of your hand. Imagine you are sitting round a table with bottles and glasses on it. Don't *upset* them!
- *Medium sized* gestures: If you speak to an audience of ten to fifteen, use fingers, hands or forearm *according* to the rhythm and the importance of the key words of your speech.
- Strong gestures: The larger the audience, the more *expansive* your gestures may be. Strong gestures come from the shoulders. Priests and politicians, for example, open their arms when they greet the audience as if to *embrace* the whole *assembly*.

Gesten
Handteller
umstoßen
mittelgroß
gemäß
ausladend
umarmen
Versammlung

What not to do

There are some movements you should *avoid* because the audience might interpret them as signs of *indecision* or arrogance:

- Don't *shrug* or pull up your shoulders.
- Don't *draw* your head *in*.
- Don't *throw* your head *back*.
- Don't cross your arms over your chest.

vermeiden
Unschlüssigkeit
zucken
einziehen
zurückwerfen

Learn from the masters. The best way to become aware of how your arms and hands can *convey meaning* is to watch actors and politicians on TV. Don't listen, just watch them with the *volume* turned down. You will be surprised to see how often they move their shoulders, arms and hands. Try to guess what they express by their gestures.

vermitteln
Bedeutung, Inhalt
Lautstärke

Going International

How to say "To your health" in the language of your business partner

Finnish	Kippis!
Hindi	Aanand!
Hebrew	L'Chayim!
Irish Gaelic	Slainte!
Maori	Kia-Ora!
Urdu	Sanda Bashi!
Welsh	Icchyd da!
Zulu	Oogy wawa!

Chapter 13

A vote of thanks

Tom Stow (**S**) sitting next to Georg (**G**). During the speech they talk to each other.

S: It's a strange feeling to be sitting here listening to a speech about my leaving the company forever.
G: Oh, I'm sure you will visit us from time to time.
S: I hope so. But what am I going to say now? I'll have to make a reply.
G: Don't worry! You can mention that you haven't felt like part of a machine. That you'll miss the company, but not too much. Look, I've even got a short proverb which suits the occasion.

Some niceties to build into a farewell speech

To your colleague:
Sixty-five. That's the age when you have acquired enough experience to lose your job.

To your partner:
Peter Bistro is a man who's always believed that honesty is the best policy and that money isn't everything. Mind you, he's been wrong about other things, too.

To your employee:
Dear Dobson, you're a man who – forty years ago – started at the bottom of the ladder … and stayed there.

(*) Dr Stow's reply on his retirement (*)

Dr Stow rises, taps his glass and begins with Georg's proverb.

Ladies and Gentlemen,
There is an Eastern proverb that says, "In the hum of the market there is money, but under the cherry tree there is rest." Well, I have been in the hum of the market for a good long time. There is a cherry tree in my garden, and it is to my garden that I intend to retire – I did not say rest!
It is difficult for me to realise that today I am leaving this firm where I have worked for so many years. I shall, I think, be quite happy without my work – and, in spite of Dr Naston's kind words, I have not the slightest doubt that the company will get along pretty well without me. I was going to say that I have been only a cog in the machine, but I think a happier and more accurate description would be a member of a team. The small part I have played in this team has been made easy for me by the loyal co-operation I have always received from every member. And it is the thought of leaving this team that makes parting rather difficult for me.
Of course, there are things I'll miss. For example researching in the archives for patents, trade marks and inventions. And I shall find it difficult to live without the constant complaints of the staff. Still, all joking aside, it has been a rewarding as well as demanding career.
Now my innings has come to an end, but I shall watch the future achievements of the team from a seat in the pavilion. You have given me a splendid souvenir to take with me, and I shall always prize this gift and what it stands for. I appreciate that you have chosen as a present my very first flop, the first patent I ever applied for at this company: the Ruvlet 200 gear transmission. What more could I want to accompany me in the twilight of my days. Thank you for your kind offering and especially for the kind wishes that have come with it – and good luck to you all!

Working with the language

Task 1: Key words in business

.... to retire	*beabsichtigen, in den Ruhestand zu treten*
the .... of the market	*das geschäftige Summen des Markts*
a .... in the machine	*ein Rädchen in der Maschine*
.... loyal co-operation from	*treue Mitarbeit von jemandem erfahren*
the .... of a team	*die Leistungen einer Mannschaft*
.... in the archives	*in den Archiven forschen*
.... for a patent	*ein Patent anmelden*
.... of the staff	*Beschwerden des Personals*

Task 2: Thinker's corner

1. Where does Dr Stow use irony?
2. Why is he not happy with the image of the "cog in a machine"?
3. What is Dr Stow's main approach in his reply to the toast?
4. What is the meaning of the imagery with "Now my innings has come to an end, but I shall watch the future achievements of the team from a seat in the pavilion."?

Great opening lies

This'll be a short speech.
I'll only talk for about five minutes.
To cut a long story short.

What to say on your own retirement

You have no idea, Ladies and Gentlemen, how wonderful it feels, knowing that forty-five busy people have turned up here this evening just to see me quit.

Ⓢ Spice up your speeches

Quotes and clichés for your reply to a farewell speech

Trennung läßt die Liebe wachsen.	Absence makes the heart grow fonder.
Auch die besten Freunde müssen einmal scheiden.	Even the best friends must part.
Ein Abschied schmerzt immer, auch wenn man sich schon lange darauf freut. (A. Schnitzler)	Leaving is also painful even if you've been eagerly waiting for it.
Wen wir am meisten lieben, für den finden wir nur wenig Worte.	Whom we love best, to them we can say least.
Es ist erstaunlich, wie nett die Menschen zu dir sind, wenn sie wissen, daß du fortgehst.	It's amazing how nice people are to you when they know you are going away. (Michael Arlen)
Der beste Zeitpunkt, an deine Pensionierung zu denken, ist, bevor dein Chef daran denkt.	The best time to start thinking about your retirement is before the boss does.
Ruhestand bedeutet doppelt soviel Ehemann/Ehefrau bei halbem Gehalt.	Retirement means twice as much husband/wife on half as much money.
Die Zeit des Abschiednehmens ist gekommen.	The time has come to say good-bye.
Jedes Fest geht mal zu Ende. Darum sage ich, es ist Zeit, meine Freunde, es ist Zeit.	Every party must come to an end. And so I'll say it's time, my friends, it's time.

Task 3: Spot the mistakes and correct them

1. It is to my garden that I intend to retire – I haven't said rest!
2. It is difficult for me to realise that today I leave this firm.
3. I have no doubt the company gets along pretty well without me.
4. I was going to say that I was only a cog in the machine.
5. I am thinking a happier and more accurate description would be a member of a team.

Task 4: Odd man out

In which sentence is "*It is* ..." not used for emphasis?

1. It is to my garden that I intend to retire.
2. It is difficult for me to realise that today I am leaving this firm where I have worked for so many years.
3. It is the thought of leaving this team that makes parting rather difficult.

Task 5: Modify your statements

Modifiers are words that soften a statement.
Do you remember the words Dr Stowe used in his speech?

1. I shall, I think, be *(ganz)* happy without my work.
2. I have not the slightest doubt that the company will get along *(recht/ziemlich)* well without me.
3. And it is the thought of leaving this team that makes parting *(ziemlich)* difficult for me.

What to say to the retiring colleague

Dear Peter, when we heard you were about to retire we passed round the hat to collect money for a nice present. Not only did we not raise any money ... but somebody even stole the bloody hat.

What to say on your own retirement

You know you're getting old when someone compliments you on your snake-skin shoes – and you're barefoot.

Task 6: Test your synonyms

Tick off the words which have the same meaning as the one in *italics*.

1. I shall always *prize* this gift and what it stands for.

☐ value
☐ esteem
☐ estimate

2. I have only been a *cog* in the machine.

☐ wheel
☐ disk
☐ part

3. The small *part* I have played in this team has been made easy for me.

☐ function
☐ role
☐ share

4. Thank you for your kind *offering* and especially for the kind wishes that have come with it.

☐ gift
☐ donation
☐ giving

5. I have not the slightest *doubt* that the company will get along pretty well without me.

☐ uncertainty
☐ hesitation
☐ disbelief

Ⓑ Building your speeches: More effective openers

1. **Thanking your host for his flattering introduction**
   Thank you for that kind introduction. It seems that I shall now have to say two prayers for forgiveness: the first for my host for telling so many lies in praising me; the second for myself – for enjoying it so much.

2. **Quotable quotes**
   A quotation is both a good entry and exit. There are lots of dictionaries to provide you with quotes that will fit your theme. But don't use quotes to show off what you know. If you have forgotten the name of the author, try this: *"A famous person once said"* … or *"It has been said that …"*.

4. **The joke**
   It's effective but dangerous. First, it must be exactly on target for your message; second, it must suit the audience and the occasion; third, it can be a catastrophe if it falls flat and nobody laughs.

5. **Complimenting the audience** (Captatio benevolentiae)
   Ladies and Gentlemen, your presence proves that there are still many people who are ready to take responsibility for our environment.

For more openings see chapter 2.

✔ Checkpoint: Preparing a reply

On such occasions you will realise that you must reply in a few words. Your audience expects a spontaneous speech with references to what the previous speaker has said. You hardly have time to prepare this, so it must be kept simple and honest.
However, you can prepare the beginning and the end. It is normal to start off with a thank-you to the host and a humorous statement. Have some profound thoughts ready for the end.
As far as the middle goes, an anecdote or story always fits. Of course, your listeners are also interested how you are going to live the last stage of your life.

Speaker's corner: Get your timing right

A speech is like a well-kept *lawn* – short and neat – how short *depends* on the *occasion*, on the hour and on your *audience*. If you are invited to make a speech, you should ask the *host*. He prepares the *agenda* and knows the audience. Here are a few *guidelines*:

Rasen
abhängen; Anlaß
Publikum
Gastgeber
Tagesordnung
Richtlinien

1. **Informal speeches:** Some speakers and most listeners would *approve* of the rule among certain *tribes* in Africa. Their procedure is that when a man rises to speak he must stand on one foot while *delivering his speech*. The minute the lifted foot touches the ground, the speech ends – or the speaker is *silenced* by force.

billigen
Stämme
eine Rede halten
zum Schweigen bringen

2. **Lunchtime engagements:** Your speech should be sharp and *witty* – particularly if everyone has to go back to work afterwards. It shouldn't last for more than five minutes.

geistreich

3. **Toasts:** They should create a *sense of community* so that everybody is able to join you in the toast. It should last two to three minutes.

Gemeinschaftsgefühl

4. **After-dinner speeches** at the end of a pleasant evening of wining and dining can be more robust in tone. Don't talk for more than five to ten minutes.

It's better to be *brief* and funny than to speak for half an hour with no laughs. No one ever complained of a speech being too short!

kurz

In this book you will find humorous stories or *suitable quotations* for most situations. You can change the places, products and professions to suit the occasion.

passendes Zitat

...pter 14

What to say at weddings

G: (*On the telephone*) Hello, Grosleger speaking.

S: Jeff Spencer here. From Quality Control. I need your advice.

G: Sure. What can I do for you?

S: Friday, next week my department will be having a party. One of my tasks is to congratulate one of our colleagues on his forthcoming marriage. Can you help me with the speech if I send you the details?

G: Okay. No problem. I'll send you some nice lines to choose from.

S: Oh, that's a great relief. Thank you very much indeed.

Some lines for Jeff's speech

Best wishes for a happy and successful first marriage.

Here's to the beautiful bride:
No matter how old you are, you don't look it.

Here's to love –
the only fire for which there's no insurance.

(*) Congratulations on a forthcoming wedding (*)

The colleagues from the Quality Control Department have met in the Red Lion, a pub just round the corner from Ruver. Jeff Spencer bangs his glass on the bar:

Colleagues, Dear Colleagues, and you Carol,
Could I have your attention for a moment? Thank you. Of course, you all know the reason for our little get-together. And a very pleasant occasion it is, too. But before I get down to business, I'd like to tell you a little story about our hero tonight, Jim Slipper. Jim and me have known each other privately for several years. Mostly it was on account of our playing squash together after work. On one occasion we were having a tiny drop of something a bit stronger watching the other squash players. There was this young creature, a real charmer, playing at a good level. "She's not bad", grunted Jim. "But she couldn't beat a man." This girl happened to be my cousin, so I fixed a game with her for Jim. He lost and when I say lost, I mean lost. Lost and won. Jim's been playing this fish ever since. You win some, you lose some, but finally he's landed the big one. Or has she landed him? Well, we'll never know. And what does it matter?
As you will have realised I am well acquainted with both the bride-to-be and the groom. I don't have a crystal ball, none of us do, except of course, the Great Spirit in the heavens. Who really knows what the future holds! I certainly don't, but I am certain that Jim and Carol do have what it takes to give each other a good run for their money.
And so all this talk of sport brings me back to our matter here. Jim and Carol will be taking a jump into the deep end, into the unknown. Next Saturday is the great day. I'd like to take this opportunity to wish them luck from the bottom of my heart. And to seal these wishes with a gift, a small statuette of two squash players doing their very best. To the future bride and ... Good health!

⊛ Carol's reply to Jeff's congratulatory speech ⊛

It's not very usual for the future bride to reply. And Jim realised just how nervous I was a few minutes ago, when he asked the wine waiter to recommend something that goes well with fingernails. But since Jeff is a close friend and also a squash partner I decided to do it.
Well, I have to start off by saying that I'm totally overwhelmed by this gift and by your warm words, Jeff. And yes, I remember how Jim and myself met on the squash court and that you were instrumental in bringing us together. What I don't remember is winning in the game, but I guess you allowed yourself some poetic licence. Still, all joking aside, your allusions to sport are apt. Over the last few years we've done many things together. And, of course, you're right, nobody can read the future, but we know each other well, so we decided it's time to take the plunge. Perhaps Jim will come out a new man, but speaking personally, I am quite satisfied with the old one. Thank you again for everything on behalf of myself and my future husband. And thank you very much for this nice gift.

Time for a smile

By the time a man learns to read women like a book,
he's too old to start a library.

Working with the language

Task 1: Key words in business

.... to business	*zur Sache kommen*
.... a contract	*einen Vertrag an Land ziehen*
be .... with a matter	*mit etwas vertraut sein*
give someone a good .... his money	*jemandem etwas für sein Geld bieten*
.... into the	*ins kalte Wasser springen*
be .... doing something	*bei etwas hilfreich sein*

Task 2: Thinker's corner

1. What theme does the speaker use to link his relationship to Jim?
2. Can you find any example of paraphrase where somebody is described in other words?
3. Why does Carol mean by, "We decided to take the plunge"?

Task 3: How to refer to the occasion

1. You all know the .... for our little .... – ....
2. And a very pleasant .... it is, too.
3. I'd like to take this .... to wish them luck from the bottom of my heart.

Task 4: How to characterise the occasion

1. Promotion, wedding:	this .... occasion	
2. Inauguration, ribbon cutting:	this .... occasion	
3. Funeral, death:	this .... occasion	

(!) Some lines to build into your speeches

Advice to the couple
Love doesn't make the world go round.
It's what makes the ride worthwhile.

Never do anything in bed that you can't pronounce.

Advice to the bride
Before marriage, a man will lie awake all night
thinking about something you said.
After marriage, he'll fall asleep before you finish saying it.

Advice to the bridegroom
You have to realise, as a man, that in any marriage there can only ever be one boss. So do exactly as she tells you, and you'll be fine.

Lines for the bride's father

The truth behind this marriage is quite simple. About a year ago, I was working out the family budget and I suddenly realised ... one of us would have to go. I chose Carol.

Carol told me, the only regret she has about getting married is leaving her mother.
I said, "No problem darling, take her with you ... please."

Lines for the bride

The bride's toast:
Here's to the men I've loved
And here's to the men I've kissed.
And here's my profound apologies
To all the men I've missed.

Lines for the bridegroom

A man in love is incomplete until he is married.
Then he is finished.

Toasts

A toast to love and laughter and happily ever after.

To keep your marriage brimming
in the ever-loving cup
Whenever you're wrong, admit it ...
whenever you're right, shut up!

May their joys be as deep as the ocean
And their misfortunes as light as the foam.

Ⓢ Spice up your speeches

Creating a link

Good speakers take up a theme or a figure of speech from the previous speaker and change or expand it. Thus both speeches form a whole and the atmosphere and the effect are intensified. This is how Carol and Jeff did it.

Jeff: Jim and Carol will be taking a *jump into the deep end,* into the unknown.
Carol: We decided it's time *to take the plunge.*

The use of paraphrases

Speakers sometimes use figures of speech or paraphrases

- to arouse interest,
- to avoid every day language
- or to make their listeners think.

Task 5: Find the spices

Do you remember how Jeff paraphrased the words in *italics*?

1. On one occasion we were having a *whiskey.*
2. There was *Carol*, a real charmer, playing at a good level.
3. *I'm not a prophet*, none of us *is*, except of course, *God*.

Time for a smile

When Lucy introduced her future husband to her parents, her mother took her aside and whispered into her ear. "Isn't he a bit too old for you? And he is completely bald." – "You needn't whisper, mother," replied Lucy, "he is almost deaf, too."

Speaker's corner: A final word on wedding speeches

At a wedding *the convention is* to tell a humorous story about the bride or *bridegroom's* childhood. Use only material that you can *deliver* comfortably. But don't *drag* a story *in* because it has amused you, especially if it has nothing to do with the occasion; and *beware of* an *improper* story which might shock the bride's father or mother.
You could start with a few words about your attitude to wedding speeches in general, whether you like them or not, and why.
If you're not *at ease* with comic material, you might want to offer some *advice* as to how to succeed in a happy marriage. Or you quote one of the experienced experts on marriage: "The love you give is the love you keep. Which is nothing. *Unless* it's divided by two."

And you could end your speech with some *witty* wishes for the young couple or a surprise toast. What about these *puns*?
"And finally, may the happy couple *lie, steal* and *cheat* ... (Pause, ... then explain).
May they *lie* in each other's arms, may they *steal away* for a *blissful* honeymoon, and may they cheat time to live as long as possible."
Remember that no one is going to listen all that *attentively* – their minds will be on the rest of the *proceedings*. Your role is, very often, just to be *jolly* and fit in with the occasion.

es ist üblich
Bräutigam
vermitteln
an den Haaren herbeiziehen
sich hüten vor; unschicklich
sich wohl fühlen
Rat
es sei denn
geistreich
Wortspiele
lügen, stehlen
betrügen
liegen; sich davonstehlen, selig
aufmerksam
Verfahren; lustig

The product launch

Meanwhile back to Georg (G) and his problems. His first year at Ruver passed quickly. It had started well, but in the last quarter of the year things were not going so smoothly. One or two speeches had gone down badly and some top managers were dissatisfied with his PR work. Georg was feeling in a meditative mood when the phone rang. It's Mr Johnson (J), the divisional leader of Off-Roader Sales.

G: Hello, Grosleger speaking.
J: Hello, this is Johnson from the Off-Roader division. In January of next year, that means in eight weeks, we're going to launch our top of the range, the new Overlander.
G: Sounds like a big occasion.
J: It certainly will be. And you'll be playing a major part in it.
G: You need a speech!
J: I certainly do and it's the central speech for the product launch itself. I've listed up the main sections and I'll send you a dossier with what we want included.

What you should not say to the presenter

Your presentation has been most entertaining.
Are there any hard facts to follow?

(*) Presenting the Overlander to the press (*)

In the main foyer of Ruver, the Overlander is located on the slope of a simulated hillside. There are illuminated arrows pointing to various new and interesting features on the jeep. The trade press are present. Mr Johnson begins to speak:

Ladies and Gentlemen, Honoured Gentlemen and Ladies from the press and not to forget them, my Colleagues from Ruver,
We are gathered here to celebrate Ruver's latest technological achievement, the Overlander, the right off-roader at the right time, and at the same time to celebrate our company itself.
Allow yourselves a few minutes, Honoured Visitors, to cast your eyes over a fine horse of a car as it conquers terrestrial opponents. (*Pause*) Not a cart-horse, not a work-horse, but a thoroughbred. Please take your time to appreciate its elegance. While you do just that, I'll describe what I'm going to talk about.
My first comment is that I'm going to keep it short. I'll give you a brief history of the product, the key word being "brief", next our aims, and markets. You'll want to know about features, in fact, I'm sure you're burning to know about them, and finally a few words to the staff who made it all work.
And now, if I could have your attention, a few historical facts on the road to this particular piece of perfection. As most of you know it all began four years ago. Customers needed something more, something else. Potential clients were polled in the biggest campaign we have ever undertaken. As a result we hammered together specs which really hit the target. Our best brains were called up for service, engineering, marketing, sales, customer service, to mention just a few. Of course, there were teething problems, as is always the case in an ambitious project. But as every good team we were able to overcome them. That brings us to where we are now.
Now what did I say was my next point? Ah yes! Objectives and markets. To put it in a nutshell, the Overlander is targeted at all markets from China through to Europe. As regards objectives, it's our aim to sell them everywhere and offer the customer reliable after sales. I guess we won't

have any problems to do that. Just look at this machine. I ask you! This all brings me to what you've all been waiting for. The features, the vehicle itself. Where should I begin? I'll go from the general down to the detail. First of all it's a four-wheel drive, but with all the comfort of on-road handling. Just look at the form. You've got that famous, solid look, a hallmark of all Ruver technology. It's a thoroughbred.

The driver has it good, too. He or she, let's not forget the ladies, sits high in a commanding driving position. So basically you've got secure off-road handling with the comfort of the on-road luxury car market.

What about the features? Ladies and Gentlemen, I sense you're getting impatient. I would be, too. Overlander includes ABS. This monitors wheels 250 times per second and adjusts the braking pressure. You can steer round any problems. That famous old "elk" test becomes nothing more than a donkey walk, mere child's play. And there's ETC, Electronic Traction Control; it applies braking force and spreads the power to the wheels with the most grip. A few more letters for you, HDC. You don't slip down hills any more. It's Hill Descent Control. Your speed is automatically cut to 7 m.p.h. Safe as houses.

Safety is vital for all of us. We've done more than one hundred crash tests including frontal tests at 40 m.p.h. You're safe from the side, too. Side impact beams. Our door latches are 250 per cent stronger than the law requires. And there are many other things. We'll go into all that later.

Finally, I'd just like to – and I know you'll agree with me – say a few words of praise for the staff who have put their backs into the making of this product, from concept through to the distribution and sales, people who are rearing to go. A big thank-you to all of you. But now back from horses and on to horse power. The Overlander is … (*fades out*)

Time for a smile

At the end of a presentation, the chairman rose and said,
"Your presentation has not left me any the wiser."
The presenter retorted, "Perhaps not wiser, sir,
but better informed."

Working with the language

Task 1: Key words in business

.... a product	*ein Produkt einführen*
the .... of the	*das Flaggschiff der Produktpalette*
play a .... *part* in	*eine bedeutende Rolle spielen*
the .... technological	*die neueste technologische Errungenschaft*
get .... to .... tacks	*zur Sache kommen*
the .... of a product	*die Eigenschaften eines Produkts*
.... clients	*potentielle Kunden befragen*
the Overlander is .... at all markets	*der Overlander ist für alle Märkte bestimmt*
offer the customer reliable .... –	*dem Kunden zuverlässigen Kundendienst anbieten*
a .... of technology	*ein Gütesiegel für Technik*
the car is as safe as	*das Auto ist absolut sicher*
safety is	*Sicherheit ist lebenswichtig*
.... the target	*das Ziel erreichen/treffen*
an .... project	*ein ehrgeiziges Projekt*
these are .... problems	*dies sind lediglich Kinderkrankheiten*

Task 2: Thinker's corner

1. Why does Mr Johnson compare the Overlander to a horse?
2. How often does the speaker use animal images?
   - ☐ twice
   - ☐ four times
   - ☐ six times
   - ☐ seven times
3. How does the speaker concentrate the listeners' attention to the car?
4. Which image is used to show that there are always problems in the beginning phase of a project?

Task 3: Guiding the listeners' attention

Can you fill in the gaps from memory?

1. Please .... your time to appreciate its elegance.
2. .... yourselves a few minutes, Honoured Visitors, to cast your eyes over this fine horse of a car.
3. And now, if I could .... your ...., a few historical facts.

Task 4: How to structure your speech

Guided translation

1. We *(versammeln)* here to celebrate our latest *(Errungenschaft)*.
2. I *(beschreiben)* what I *(reden werde)* about.
3. I *(gebe)* you a *(kurz)* history of the product.
4. I *(gehe)* from the general *(zum)* the detail.
5. And there are many other things. We *(kommen dazu)* all that *(später)*.

Task 5: How to be brief

1. My first comment is that I'm going to *k......* it *s........t*.
2. To ..... it in a *n..........l*, the Overlander is targeted at all markets.
3. Our best brains were called up for service, engineering, marketing, sales, customer service, to *m........n* just a ....

(B) Building your speeches

The outline of Mr Johnson's speech

1. introduction
2. a little history of the product
3. the objectives, markets
4. new features
5. comment on the staff
6. conclusion about product (not included)

Giving an overview

Ich würde meiner Präsentation gerne einen Überblick über das Projekt voranstellen.	I'd like to begin my presentation by giving you an overview of the project.
Meine Präsentation gliedert sich in drei Teile.	My presentation will be in three main parts.
Ich werde drei Hauptbereiche behandeln.	I'll be covering three main areas.
Ich werde Ihnen die wichtigsten Stufen unseres Projekts schildern.	I'll be developing the major stages of our project.
Ich werde Ihnen kurz den Werdegang des Produkts schildern.	I'll give you a brief history of the product.
Ich werde vom Allgemeinen zum Besonderen gehen.	I'll go from the general down to the detail.
Im ersten Teil meiner Präsentation werde ich …	In the first part of my presentation I'll …
Im zweiten Teil unserer Besprechung ist Zeit für Diskussion und Fragen.	Then, in the second part of the meeting, there will be a period for free discussion and question time.
Zuerst würde ich gerne … Zweitens könnten wir … Und ich werde schließen mit …	Firstly, I'd like to … Secondly, we could … And I'll finish with …
Zuerst gebe ich Ihnen einen Überblick über … Dann werde ich … Schließlich …	First, I'll give you an overview of … Then I'll … Lastly …
Damit ist mein Überblick abgeschlossen.	That completes my overview.
Alles in allem wird das ungefähr … Minuten in Anspruch nehmen.	Altogether this will take about … minutes.
Ich stehe Ihnen am Schluß gerne für Fragen zur Verfügung.	I'll be happy to answer any questions at the end.

Ⓢ Spice up your speeches

How to dramatise your speech

Mr Johnson creates interest or suspense by suggesting that the audience senses a need to know more about the Overlander.

1. You'll want to know about features ...
2. Ladies and Gentlemen, I sense you're getting impatient. I would be, too.
3. I'm sure you're burning to know about them.

How to develop your imagery

It's not the number of different images or metaphors that count in a speech. Good speakers take one image and develop it in the course of their talk.

This is what Mr Johnson does. He chooses a horse, the noblest, the thoroughbred because it can get into places where an ordinary horse can't.

1. Cast your eyes over this fine horse of a car as it conquers terrestrial opponents.
2. It's a thoroughbred

Mr Johnson compares it to other less noble horses and to a donkey to emphasise the efficiency and elegance of the Overlander.

3. Not a work-horse, not a cart-horse.
4. That famous old "elk" test becomes nothing more than a donkey walk.

And he uses the animal imagery in a wordplay to link up parts of his speech.

5. But now back from horses and on to horse power.

And he keeps to his imagery to draw the attention to the staff who are rearing, waiting impatiently to go on with the next part.

6. I'd just like to say a few words of praise for the staff who are rearing to go.

Speaker's corner: How to involve your listeners

Ask the right questions. There are three types of questions you can use in a presentation. Each allows you to *obtain* a deeper level of *involvement*.

erreichen; Anteilnahme

Rhetorical questions

They will keep your listeners active and thinking. This is especially *valuable* when you don't have time or it' s not *appropriate* actually to discuss an *issue*. Mr Johnson uses two types of questions. The first is a rhetorical one. With the other two he *pretends* to forget how to continue. The audience is expecting an *awkward* silence and is pleasantly surprised.

wertvoll
passend
Frage
vorgeben
peinlich

1. What about the features? 2. Where should I begin? 3. Now what did I say was my next point? Ah yes!

Involvement questions

Ask for a show of hands to get listeners more involved and to give you a quick way to *gauge* their reactions. "Who has ever driven an off-road car?"

abschätzen, beurteilen

Ask for a *volunteer*

Freiwilliger

Have a *volunteer* from the group help you in your demonstration. "Who would like to climb into the driver's seat for a short demonstration?" Even though only one person speaks or acts, you can feel the adrenaline *rush* through the others as they consider whether they might volunteer.

hier: strömen

Choice of language

You can roughly break down your listeners into three different types. In the next chapter we'll discuss how to *appeal* to all types by the *choice* of your words.

ansprechen: Wahl

Chapter 16

Motivating the workforce

Two trade union members, Dave (**D**) and Tony (**T**), are discussing the speech of Mrs Grant, the union representative. She is just about to begin to speak.

D: Well, we'll see what's going to happen now. Mrs Grant looks very nervous. I don't know if a woman should be doing that job.

T: I bet she'll be talking about the wild cat strike that some of the workers have called. There's a lot of support for it.

D: Yes, and that's bad for the trade union and bad for Mrs Grant.

A speech opener

Ladies and Gentlemen,
Since June 1972 you have survived ...
one year, eight months of Edward Heath,
two years of Harold Wilson,
three years of James Callaghan,
eleven and a half year of Margaret Thatcher,
six years, six months of John Major,
and two years of Tony Blair ...,
so I'm sure you'll be able to put up
with thirty minutes of me!

⊛ Warning against an unofficial strike ⊛

Mr Chairman and Comrades,

I won't beat about the bush. Straight to the point. As you know there are calls for an unofficial strike as a reaction to the intended dismissals by Ruver. Happened very quickly, I must say, none of us expected it. But now it has become absolutely clear that we must act swiftly, and swiftly and decisively we will act. We owe this to our members who have been loyal to this movement over long years. And they know why they have stood to us. The reason, my friends, is that our members know we will stand up for them and their rights in all labour disputes.

And what about this unofficial strike? Some comrades have called on workers to come out on a wild cat strike. I ask you, a wild cat strike? Such behaviour, fellow workers, is nothing more than pulling the carpet from under our feet, by "our" I mean your official trade union. I tell you we won't take it lying down. Of one thing you can be sure. These wild cat leaders will not be there later to negotiate for you, to put in the hours of work, to build bridges to a management which may not care. What action, you will ask, do we intend to take?

Well, first we must look the problem squarely in the eye. Fact is management are trying to rationalise workplaces away. We've been expecting it. And we've prepared our arguments well. So well, that they'll hold water in any weather. So first, let's go public, let's go to the press and show the world where we stand. Brothers and Sisters, let us not go blindly on strike, let's keep our powder dry instead of shooting it at the first attack from our management rivals. Rather we should list up our comments and combine them into a statement which we will release to the press.

Comrades, don't follow the wild cat blindly, it will turn on you. I appeal to you men and women to follow the banner and support your official trade union. "Once more into the breach, dear Friends." Thank you!

Working with the language

Task 1: Key words in business

Do you remember these phrases?

go	*an die Öffentlichkeit gehen*
.... to the workers	*zu den Arbeitern stehen*
.... the trade union	*die Gewerkschaft unterstützen*
an argument	*ein Argument ist hieb- und stichfest*
rationalise	*Arbeitsplätze wegrationalisieren*
.... a .... to the press	*eine Presseerklärung herausgeben*
reaction to	*Reaktion auf beabsichtigte Entlassungen*
What .... shall we ....?	*Welche Maßnahme sollen wir ergreifen?*

Do you remember the prepositions?

call ...... a strike	*einen Streik ausrufen*
put ...... hours of work	*Arbeitszeit aufbringen*
stand .... one's rights	*für seine Rechte einstehen*
come .... a wild cat strike	*in einen wilden Streik treten*

Time for a smile

A company was having a problem with all the employees on a sit-down strike.
A very smart executive told the strikers that they might as well be comfortable, so he provided them with blankets and cases of brandy. When the brandy was half-consumed, the boss sent in ten young women to entertain the sit-downers. Then he brought over the strikers' wives so that they could see how comfortable their husbands were. That ended the sit-down strike.

Task 2: Thinker's corner

1. If you had to find one theme to characterise this speech what would it be?
   A. Let's fight.
   B. Let's negotiate.
   C. Let's go public.

2. From which thematic field does the speaker take most of her images?
   A. From nature
   B. From furniture
   C. From war

3. What is the trade union official's main intention?
   A. appeal to logic
   B. appeal to emotions
   C. give information

Task 3: Beef up your word power

Find the nouns.

adjective	**noun**	**noun**
loyal	....	Treue
decisive	....	Entschlossenheit
public	....	Öffentlichkeit

verb	**noun**	
dismiss	....	Entlassung
intend	....	Absicht
expect	....	Erwartung

Ⓢ Spice up your speeches

Chiasmus: A chaismus is an elegant figure of speech. A diagonal or crosswise arrangement of two parts of a sentence. It is the inversion in a second phrase or clause of the order of words in the first.

We must *act swiftly*,
and *swiftly* and decisively we will *act*.

Task 4: Fit in the spices

Say it the speaker's way.

What she might have said	... what she actually said.
Let's face the problem.	Let's ...... the problem squarely in the ......
I'll come straight to the point.	I won't ...... about the ......
Let's try to find common ground with the management.	Let's build ...... to the management.
Let's keep our eyes open and act carefully.	Let's keep our ...... dry.
Let's go to the press.	Let's go ......
Take your places and help to defend our cause.	Once more into the ......
Support the cause of the trade union.	Follow the ...... of the trade union.
Attack somebody unexpectedly.	Pull the ...... from under somebody's ......

Time for a smile

The boss was addressing a meeting of the firm's senior executives and sales staff . "Now, when my son starts to work here tomorrow," he said, "I want you to treat him just as you would treat any other employee who was going to take over the company in two year's time."

Speaker's Corner: Reaching the listeners' whole brain

Our *brain* is divided in two parts. Good speakers reach the *whole* brain of their listeners, they keep both sides busy. The left side *processes* the facts and the figures. The right side processes the way you present them: the images, the gestures and the tone of your voice that *accompany* your words. Your listeners react to these stimuli in different ways, because they belong to different types:

Gehirn
ganz
verarbeitet
begleiten

- the visual type
- the auditive type
- and the kinesthetic type.

If you want to influence all of them you have to speak on three different *wavelengths*. Your speech should be like a *mirror* in which they can *recognize* themselves so that they will pay attention and *trust* you.

Wellenlänge
Spiegel; erkennen
vertrauen

The visual listeners

When they speak they use expressions like:
Can you show me, can you give me an idea, bring some light into the dark, get a clear picture of, look at it from another *angle* etc.
With them you should use visual language, imagery, metaphores and comparisons whenever possible. Tell them about *size, shape* and colours of your product. Use concrete – not abstract – words and you will be on the same wavelength because you have a language *in common*. Give them time to see the imagery of your language before their *mind's eye*.

Blickwinkel
Größe; Form
gemeinsam
geistiges Auge

The auditive listeners

They like music and a melodious *voice* that comes deep from the *chest.* Their language has few pictures to *convey*, they *prefer* words that describe sounds and *noises*. They will use phrases like: that *sounds* interesting; I understand clearly what you mean, I want to say, an inner voice tells me that, there are *rumours*, may I summarise, I was speechless, I'm *all ears*; *mutual* understanding. If you want to make them feel at home, don't use pictures, use auditive language: sounds, noises.

Stimme
Brust
vermitteln; vorziehen; Geräusch
klingen
Gerücht
ganz Ohr, gegenseitig

The kinesthetic or emotional listeners

They are neither visual nor auditive listeners. They are not people of many words, because it is not easy for them to express *feelings*. They are often persons who *enjoy* working with their hands and feet: dancers, doctors, engineers. They prefer sports they can feel: swimming, hiking and they like *spicy* meals. They will use words that describe what you can *touch* with your hands or feel on your *skin*:
We can handle that; it feels like, I know how you feel about it, it *smells a bit fishy*, grasp, get in touch with, be under pressure, it goes under the skin; it was quite a shock for.

Gefühle
gerne etwas tun
würzig
berühren
Haut
verdächtig sein

Human beings are complex. Visual, auditive or kinesthetic types do not exist as ideal types. Most people are combinations of two or all three. So if you want to be on the safe side, *appeal* to all *senses* – to the eye of the visual type, to the ear of the auditive type and to the emotions of the kinesthetic type.

ansprechen
Sinne

Chapter 17

Presenting your thing

In the course of the last three months Ruver has been in contact with a certain inventor from Germany, Professor Otto. He has come up with an interesting invention, the Personal Parking Protector. Georg Grosleger has arranged for him to make a presentation of it to executives at Ruver.

What to say to the presenter

At the end of the presentation the chairman said to the speaker, "Miller, I wouldn't say you have told us a bag of lies, but the way you just rearranged the truth in your favour was impressive."

Excuse me, Mr Smith, but who wrote
this nonsense into your manuscript?

(*) The Personal Parking Protector (*)

Georg Grosleger introduces the speaker:

Ladies and Gentlemen,
I believe you've all received our pre-presentation documentation, so you know what the theme is today and you are acquainted with the reputation of the inventor who is related to the famous Otto of the combustion engines. So, to make it as brief as possible, may I present Professor Siegfried Otto. Sir, we await your information with excitement. Professor Otto!

The professor takes the floor:

Ladies and Gentlemen,
Of course, may I say at the outset that I'm very happy to be here today? I'm also grateful to have the possibility to speak English. I acknowledge that I'm sadly out of practice, so I ask you to bear with me and be patient.
Let me come straightaway to the reason for this presentation. We have a device for cars, no, let me correct myself, for the drivers of cars. It's P.P.P., a gadget, a time-saver, a relief for the nerves, and it's cheap. What, you may ask, do the letters stand for? No, it's not Private Patients Plan medical insurance. Much more practical. I'm talking about the Personal Parking Protector. "What's that?" you will ask. Something to keep parking areas safe? No, Dear Listeners. Indeed it is not. But perhaps I should explain with the help of this handy flipchart. Please refer to the handouts in front of you (*using a laser pointer he shoots at the first sheet*).

Here, Honourable Spectators, you can see the idea. We have that – oh so typical – situation in every town, almost in every village. We park our cars, go to do our shopping for ten minutes, return, and find our car trapped between a hundred others. You can't drive off to your next vital appointment. Totally frustrated, you phone the police. Of course, these greenbacks or green-bottles or whatever you choose to call them do not arrive. Could you now please turn your attentions to the upper right-hand corner of the flip-chart? There you have it! You get angry, nervous, and then ill. High blood pressure, any one of a thousand unhealthy things. Fellow sufferers, think of your health, think of the town's, the country's, even the continent's collective health!

Sheet 2: The Solution

Okay, that was the problem that we all know. Every cloud has a silver lining. The solution. An escape from all this stress. Cast your eyes over sheet two. Look at device D. It prevents the blocking of your parked car. Please observe. The bumper bar B is movable and can expand the length of your car. It is driven by the electrical motor M, a gear-wheel G and the tooth rack R. By the way, I see some of you are taking notes. Please don't waste your time, just refer to the handouts.

Sheet 3: *How to handle the P.P.P. in five steps*

1) *Park the car at a good distance from the car in front and behind.*
2) *Move the bumper bar out to expand the length.*
3) *Adjust the distance depending on your driving experience.*
4) *Return to your car after shopping and retract the bumper to its original position.*
5) *Drive the car out of the parking lot. Well done!*

Now I come to the central part of my presentation. Here's the future. Five simple steps. I'll just switch on the overhead projector. There it is.

And in the near future there will be a deluxe version of the P.P.P. That will have a magic eye, a special sensor which will protect you if a car wants to park too close in front of you. It reacts to intruders, the spiked bar comes out and Bob's your uncle. It's done. (*applause*)

Working with the language

Task 1: Key words for presenters

.... a presentation to	*eine Präsentation vor leitenden Angestellten halten*
.... the pre-presentation documentation	*die Präsentationsunterlagen im voraus erhalten*
.... to the handouts	*auf die Tischvorlagen verweisen*
.... on the OHP	*den Overheadprojektor einschalten*
.... with the help of a flipchart	*mit Hilfe eines Flipcharts erläutern*
.... with an interesting invention	*mit einer interessanten Erfindung aufwarten*
... . with an inventor	*mit einem Erfinder im Kontakt sein*
.... notes	*Notizen machen*
make it .... *as* possible	*es so kurz als möglich machen*

Task 2: Thinker's corner

1. What does the professor appeal to in order to influence the audience?
2. What are the three main steps of the presentation?
3. How does the professor try to keep the attention of his listeners?

Task 3: Preposition exercise

1. You are acquainted .... the reputation .... the inventor.
2. I ask you to bear .... me and be patient.
3. I acknowledge that I'm sadly .... practice.
4. What, you may ask, do the letters stand ....?
5. I'm talking .... the Personal Parking Protector.

Task 4: Guiding the attention of the audience

The words in *italics* are anagrams. Restore the original.

1. Please *runt* your attentions to the upper part of the flipchart.
2. *Scat* your eyes over sheet two.
3. Just *freer* to the handouts in front of you.
4. Please *verbose* that the bumper bar B is movable.
5. *Three* you *evah* it!

Task 5: More ways of beginning your speech

Fill in the missing words.

1. May I say at the .... that ...
2. Let's .... with ...
3. I'll .... off by dealing with ...

Task 6: Say it the speaker's way

Do you remember what the professor used for the words in *italics*?

1. You are *familiar* with the reputation of the inventor.
2. I ask you to *put up* with me and be patient.
3. I *admit* that I'm sadly out of practice.
4. What, you may ask, do the letters P.P.P. *represent*?

Time for a smile

He was testing the microphone.
"Can you hear me in that back corner?"
"Yes," came a reply, "and I will gladly change places
with somebody who can't."

(B) Building your speeches

Structure your presentation

Darf ich einleitend sagen, daß ...?	May I say at the outset that ...
Fangen wir mit ... an.	Let's start with ...
Lassen Sie mich einleitend sagen ...	To begin with, let me say ...
Ich beginne mit ...	I'll start off by dealing with ...
Betrachten wir zuerst die Vorteile.	Let us first consider the advantages.
Ich möchte zuerst etwas über ... sagen.	I'd like to start by saying something about ...
Ich möchte Ihnen zuerst eine allgemeine Vorstellung von ... geben.	First, I'd like to give you a general idea / picture of ...
Ich beginne mit einer Zusammenfassung der Probleme, die wir mit ... haben.	I'll begin by summarising the problems we're having with ...
Bevor wir zu ... kommen, könnten wir vielleicht zuerst ...?	Before we move on to ..., could we perhaps first ...?
Bevor ich fortfahre, wollen wir einmal ... betrachten.	Before we go on let's just consider ...
So viel zu den Kosten.	So much for the costs.
Und nun zum Gewinn.	Now for the profits.

Announcing the next step

Ich komme nun zum Kern meiner Präsentation.	Now I come to the central part of my presentation.
Als nächstes will ich mich auf ... konzentrieren.	Next I'd like to concentrate on ...
Der nächste Punkt, den ich behandeln möchte, ist ...	The next point I wish to deal with is ...
Wenn wir uns nun ... zuwenden.	If I could now turn to ...
Wenn es dazu keine weiteren Fragen gibt, würde ich gerne ...	If there are no further questions at this point, I'd like to ...

Gut. Nun zu unserem nächsten Punkt.	Right. Now to our next point.
Ich würde gerne zu meinem nächste(n) Thema / Punkt / Frage / Problem kommen.	I'd like to move on to my next subject / point / item / issue / problem.
Das nächste Dia erklärt …	The next slide will clarify …
Wie Sie dem folgenden Diagramm entnehmen …	As you can see in the following chart …
Könnten wir nun zum wichtigsten Grund für … kommen?	Perhaps we could pass on to the main reason for …
Kommen wir zu der Frage, warum …	Let's move on to the question of why …
Das ist also die gegenwärtige Situation. Betrachten wir nun …	So that's the present situation. Now let's look at …
Lassen Sie mich nun auf die anderen Funktionen zu sprechen kommen.	Let me now come to the other functions.

Ⓢ Spice up your speeches: Written English versus spoken English

Most people prepare their presentations in writing. The result is more often than not a written paper and not a presentation. Don't forget that your audience is doing you a favour by listening to you. They want be talked to, so don't read them a paper. Here are some rules you should observe.

- When preparing your presentation, don't copy from catalogues or specifications. They are in written English.
- Learning your presentation by heart is almost as bad as reading it to the audience.
- Use your own words and have them checked by one of the native speakers in your company or an English trainer.

Instead of A, B, C …
This intelligent household robot is one metre tall, weighs 200 kilos, has a new generation of chips, the gift of speech – to mention only a few of its functions.

… say A and B and C
Our intelligent household robot is one metre tall *and* weighs 200 kilos, *and* it has a new generation of chips *and* – most important of all – it can talk to you, *and* a lot more.

Instead of group words and the third person (he, she) …
Participants at meetings will experience how tiring it is to listen to a presentation that is read by the presenter.

… use first or second person: I, you
You are in a meeting and the speaker doesn't talk to you. He reads his paper. And what happens? *You* doze off after a few minutes. *I* think you all know what *I* mean.

Instead of abstract words ...
The user of traditional *domestic equipment* will have *encountered* disagreeable *failures*.

... use concrete words
I suppose *you* know that sort of unpleasant surprise. You bought a *cheap vacuum cleaner* and when you tried it at home it started *blowing* instead of *sucking*.

Instead of reported *speech* ...
Dr Block informed me that he would introduce a modern communication system.

... use the more lively direct speech
"You know what?" Dr Block said to me the other day, "I'm going to have this old communication system replaced by a modern one."

Use pictorial language, comparisons and analogies
Don't say inflation is expansion or increase in the quantity of money circulating, in relation to the goods available for purchase.
Compare things that have nothing to do with each other: Inflation is when wallets are getting bigger and the shopping bag smaller.

How to thank the presenter

Thank you, Mr Smith, you have presented a series of good, new ideas. Unfortunately the good ideas weren't new and the new ideas weren't any good.

Speaker's corner: Last minute preparations

The equipment
If you need a microphone, test it before the other *participants* arrive. It is very *embarrassing* to find out that the micro isn't working when you want to begin your talk. Check how to raise and lower it so that you are able to *adjust* it to your *height*. Try it out, in order to know how far away from it you need to stand. Check the OHP. Don't stand in front of the *screen* and don't turn your back towards the audience.

Teilnehmer; peinlich
anpassen; Größe
Leinwand

Outward *appearance*
First impressions are the most important. Check your clothes in front of a mirror. If you tend to put your hands in your pockets, leave your *change* and keys in a safe place so that you aren't tempted to *jangle* them. Make sure that you have a clean *handkerchief* in case you need to wipe your *brow*.

Erscheinung
Kleingeld
klimpern
Taschentuch; Stirn

Take your time
If you've worked hard to make the opening words of your speech interesting, don't waste them by starting to speak while the audience is talking and settling down in their seats. Wait for *silence*, even if it seems to take *ages*.

Ruhe
Ewigkeit

The first words
Start *confidently* and loudly so that everyone can hear what you' have to say. Whatever you do, don't be hurried. Talk slowly and make plenty of pauses so that the audience can *respond*.

selbstbewußt
reagieren

Be prepared for accidents
If anything can go wrong, it will go wrong. So do *anticipate* accidents and be prepared for them to happen. Keep smiling.

vorhersehen

Chapter 18

The after-dinner speech

Dr Koutert (**K**) is having a coffee with Tim Black (**B**), an R&D department leader.

K: So I've been asked to do the honours this evening in the restaurant of our new Academy.

B: What's the occasion?

K: Well, it's the annual convention, a public relations thing really. Today we're having a world-wide technical meeting with customers and agents from the States, Japan and the Far East. In fact most of the world but not including Europe. There may be complaints about quality and service. The Board has decided that not only should I attend the dinner, but that I should complement the dinner with an after-dinner speech. I'm not looking forward to it.

Good starters

Good evening. My name is James Kelly. I'm here to help you through your after-dinner nap.

Finally, I've been asked by the organisers to announce that, for reasons of safety, at the end of this talk you are requested to refrain from getting up on to the tables or chairs during my standing ovation. Thank you for your co-operation.

(*) Speaking to a world on wheels (*)

Dr Koutert rises and coughs to gain attention.

Gentlemen, Colleagues from the agencies, and perhaps most important Honoured Customers,

I would like to take the opportunity to round off this fine dinner and good atmosphere with a few closing words to put our meeting today into perspective. I am, of course, aware that today was a day of problem-solving and trouble-shooting, but I think I speak for all of us, when I say we have come up with a whole range of good results.

And, if I may mention it, one problem was the issue of hunger which we all felt by 6 pm today. With the help of this splendid dinner we have solved that problem, too.

That brings me to our gathering here this evening and it is a joy for me to recognise the truly international flavour of our friends here. Just look around! In the corner to my right I see our friends from Brazil, Peru, Argentina, to mention just a few South American partners, in the corner to my left we go to the other end of the world and I see China, Japan, India. Forgive me for not listing each country. And what is also fascinating, all types are represented, young and old, commercial and technical, manufacturers and customers. The chain of activities is complete. And what links us all together is this special area of technology, the automobile. For whatever reasons, we are all bound to one another by our interest in that box on four wheels. What it was in the past, what it is now, and what it will look like in the future.

We all have our ideas. But as I look around me and see half the world represented here a thought crosses my mind. We're all from different cultures, we have different priorities, different traditions. What I'm trying to say is (*pause*), I am wondering how you find our cooking, our cuisine. I could imagine it's a shock, no, more a pleasant surprise for some (*grunting in the audience*).

Let's leave these worldly pleasures for a moment to return to the realities of Ruver. The past two years have been, well, not the easiest to manœuvre. The market at present is like a raging storm. And we want to remain sea-worthy. This year we bought some companies and some bad

headaches. But with the right treatment and a healthier life style we're recovering.
And now we've come full circle. So Gentlemen, let's raise our glasses to a more peaceful, and even more fruitful time, Gentlemen, a toast to a good day's work!

Working with the language

Task 1: Key words in business

.... a dinner	*an einem Abendessen teilnehmen*
.... about quality	*Reklamationen über die Qualität*
.... the dinner with an after-dinner speech	*ein Abendessen mit einer Tischrede abrunden*
.... with a .... of good results.	*eine Reihe guter Ergebnisse erzielen*
a day of	*ein Tag des Suchens und Behebens von Fehlern*
.... a problem	*ein Problem lösen*
have	*unterschiedliche Prioritäten setzen*

Task 2: Thinker's corner

1. How does Dr Koutert keep the atmosphere light?
2. Why does he avoid jokes and humour?
3. Why does he not tell any stories or anecdotes?

Advice from the expert

One good after-dinner speech which is short and sweet to the rest of the diners is "I'll get the bill."

Task 3: Spot the mistake

1. We are all having our ideas.
2. The past two years were, well, not the easiest to manœuvre.
3. What has it (the car) been in the past, what is it now, and what will it look like in the future?
4. But as I look around me … a thought is crossing my mind.
5. I am aware today has been a day of trouble-shooting.

(B) Building an after-dinner speech

Five steps to your after-dinner speech

You can adapt Dr Koutert's phrases to quite a number of speeches. Just expand each step with a few facts and you get a good five-minute speech.

1. **Address the audience**
   Gentlemen, Colleagues from the agencies, and perhaps most important Honoured Customers …
2. **Announce your purpose**
   I would like to take the opportunity to round off this fine dinner and good atmosphere with a few closing words.
3. **Create common ground**
   I think I'm speaking for all of us, when I say we have come up with a whole range of good results.
   And what links us all together is this special area of technology, the automobile?
   We are all bound to one another by our interest in that box on four wheels.
4. **Announce the end of the speech**
   And now we've come full circle.
5. **Propose a toast**
   Gentlemen, a toast to a good day's work!

Ⓢ Spice up your speeches

Task 4: Adding some spices

1. Use a paraphrase:
   Let's leave the *world of food and drink* for a moment.
2. Do you remember the simile or image:
   The market at present is *extremely dangerous.*
3. Use a sailor's language:
   And we want to remain *competitive.*
4. Create a zeugma:
   This year we bought some companies which *caused us some bad headaches.*

Two more spices

1. How to change the subject

And, *if I may mention it,* one problem was the issue of hunger.
Let's leave these worldly pleasures for a moment *to return* to the realities of Ruver.
That brings me to another subject.
That reminds me of another problem.
Having said this we should also mention that …

2. How to seem spontaneous

Of course, Dr Koutert has prepared his speech, nevertheless he seems to be speaking off the cuff. The words of perception give the impression that he is inspired by the moment, by what he sees around him.
As I look around me and see half the world represented here *a thought crosses my mind.*
Just look around! In the corner to my right I see our friends from Brazil, Peru, Argentina, Brazil …
It is a joy for *me to recognise* the truly international flavour of our friends here.

Speaker's corner: Humour across frontiers

It has been said that humour crosses national *boundaries* with difficulty. *Serious-minded*, factual Germans do not *split their sides* on hearing American jokes about Texas, which usually depend on *gross exaggeration*. The story about the Mexican driving just as fast as he could for 24 hours to get out of Texas, but finding he had not managed it, *thrills* the American *imagination* but sounds *far fetched* to the German, who would usually reply, "He should have used a German car."

Grenzen; ernsthaft
sich kaputtlachen
grobe Übertreibung
Phantasie anregen;
weit hergeholt

Apart from the Koreans (who seem to like everybody's jokes), few Orientals are amused by American or European jokes. The Confucian and Buddhist *preoccupation* with truth, sincerity, kindliness and politeness automatically eliminates humourous techniques such as sarcasm, satire, exaggeration and parody, and finds little *merit* in crazy humour or jokes about religion, sex and underprivileged minorities. Sick or black humour is definitely out.

Beschäftigung
Sinn, Wert

So what is left, you might ask? Eastern humour, such as we understand it, is *couched in subtlety*, gentle, indirect *reproach* or *reprimand*, occasionally *victimising* listeners in a *sly* but non-aggressive manner which still leaves them room for response and stops short of *depriving* them of their *dignity*. Even the rougher, occasionally *bawdy* Koreans take great care to protect the listener's *wholeness* or *standing*.

raffiniert verpackt
Vorwurf; Tadel
aufs Korn nehmen;
listig
berauben
Würde; obszön
Integrität; Stand

Chinese are noted for their aphorisms and proverbs, and they and the Indians find great *sources* of humour in parables, which we in the west find only *moderately* funny, although they

Quellen
gemäßigt

do combine wisdom, moralising and a sense of perspective. We can understand Malaysian *tales*, while we rarely understand Japanese jokes. But then, neither do the Chinese.

Is there such a thing as a 'national style' of humour? Before answering this question directly one must accept the fact that there is such a thing as international humour – that is to say, some types of humour and some jokes gain international acceptance. In particular, this is true of *slapstick*, age-old in its use and laughed at by Europeans, Americans, Africans and Orientals *alike*. It is very much *in evidence*, for instance, on Japanese television. There seems to be a general love of *witnessing violence*, which may compensate, in the international arena, for not always being allowed to practise it. There are also 'international' jokes repeated across many *borders*, such as the one about 'who must jump out of the aeroplane first', elephant jokes, restaurant jokes and *hilarious* stories about golfers.

Richard D. Lewis, When cultures collide. Nicholas Brealy Publishing, London, p. 20ff.

Erzählungen

Klamauk; primitiver Humor

gleichermaßen; feststellbar

sehen; Gewalt

Grenzen

lustig

How to end your after-dinner speech

Now that we've all enjoyed a wonderful meal, I'd like to remind you that wild, uninhibited applause burns up twenty-five calories a minute! So start burning! Cheers.

Chapte

Interview for a new job

At the Red Lion, a pub just round the corner from Ruver. Georg is drinking a Guinness with Dr Koutert.

K: Georg, I can tell you we're all sorry to see you go. Perhaps you should rethink your strategy. I'm sure the boss could find you something that would suit you.

G: No, thanks anyway, but I've set my mind on something new. By the way, I've got an interview at ICE.

K: The chemical company? Good! Well I wish you every success.

Communication problems

The bar of the Hotel Montezuma was crowded.
As there was only one empty chair at the table of an elderly
Mexican businessman James bowed and said,
"Kelly, James Kelly." The gentleman rose, bowed and said,
"Buenos Dias."
The next morning James met the Mexican at breakfast. He
bowed and said, "Buenos dias."
James smiled and replied, "Kelly, James Kelly."
When James met the friendly gentleman at lunchtime,
the same ceremony happened again.
The waiter who was serving them explained to James,
"Buenos dias is not the name, you understand. He is only saying
'Good morning'." James was grateful and when he met the
Mexican again at dinner, he said, "Buenos dias."
The Mexican, pleased to see that James had taken the trouble
to learn the language replied, "Kelly, James Kelly."

(*) Back to the world of persuasion (*)

Mr Newman (**N**) *at ICE is running the interview with Georg Grosleger* (**G**).

N: (*fade in*) Fine, Mr Grosleger, as you know I've read your CV and other documentation. But actually, I'd like to ask you just in a few words to give me some information about yourself and your reasons for changing to us at ICE. After all, you've got a good job at Ruver.

G: Yes, thank you. Well, I have to say you're right. I do have a good job at Ruver, and they're willing to offer me more.
The gist of it is that I need success not only in terms of statistics but also psychologically. And in my heart of hearts I feel I need new challenges. In a way I landed a good job and a stomach ache. The problem was the red tape.
If I could describe my history briefly to you. Well, back in Germany I studied advertising. I always liked to work with visuals in larger projects, if possible. But then at BWM in Germany I got a job as an assistant to the Board. Doing a thousand general jobs. Was it a mistake? I don't know. It changed my career direction.
Then there was a rationalisation programme. I lost my job. I decided I wanted to try foreign places and England was the first choice. I know, I know, before you say anything, England is not foreign, but for me it was. It was a question of getting used to things.
Here I took over a department at Ruver. Actually, it was in the field of public relations so it was more up my street. But, to come back to your question, I feel that that type of work was not quite right for me. So basically I took the risk, took a shot at it and when I saw your advertisement, I went for it.
To return to your question why am I interested in chemicals, why am I applying for this position, indeed, why this interview? To tell you the truth, the answer is that it could give me a chance to get back to the roots – real advertising whether it's chemicals or motor cars, that's all the same to me. It's a chance to create, build up advertising and advertising campaigns. To work in the world of persuasion ....

Working with the language

Task 1: Key words in business

.... someone's CV	jemandes Lebenslauf lesen
.... one's strategy	seine Vorgehensweise überdenken
.... a good job	eine gute Stelle ergattern
need new	neue Herausforderungen benötigen
get a job as an .... to the	den Posten eines Direktionsassistenten bekommen
.... a department at Ruver	eine Abteilung bei Ruver übernehmen
.... a position	sich für einen Posten bewerben
...... the .... of public relations	auf dem Gebiet der Öffentlichkeitsarbeit
.... one's job	seinen Arbeitsplatz verlieren
.... to another company	zu einer anderen Firma wechseln

Task 2: Say it the speaker's way

Do you remember Georg's exact words?

What he might have said ...	... and in fact did say.
Deep down in my heart I feel I need new challenges	.... I feel I need new challenges.
This position *suits me better.*	This position ....
It could give me a chance to get back to *my professional origins.*	It could give me a chance to get back ....
Quite honestly, the answer is yes.	...., the answer is yes.
It doesn't make any difference to me.	.... to me.
I *got* a good job and a *problem.*	I .... a good job and a ....

Task 3: Two ways of saying it

George said it twice, but in different words. Can you do it?

I took *a shot at* it.	I .... it.
To come back to your question.	.... to your question.
It's a chance to *create* advertising.	It's a chance to .... advertising.

Task 4: Did you get the message?

Which expression comes closest to what Georg wanted to say?

1. The *gist of it* is that I need success.
A. the problem
B. the most important reason
C. the obvious reason

2. The problem was the *red tape.*
A. working climate
B. lack of professionalism
C. excessive bureaucracy

3. But *actually*, I'd like to ask you to give me some information about yourself.
A. as a matter of fact
B. presently
C. today

4. It could give me a chance to get *back to the roots.*
A. back to Germany
B. back to what I have been trained for
C. back to the chemical industry

Misunderstanding at a meeting

The Chairman interrupted his speech.
"Now, Dobson, this is not a kindergarten. Order! Order!"
Whereupon Dobson replied quietly,
"Okay, I'll have a cheese sandwich then."

Speaker's corner: The problem of eye contact

Eye contact is the most important skill in communication. It's not enough just to look at people – good eye contact means to know where to look and how long to *maintain* the eye contact.

Blickkontakt
aufrechterhalten

The length of the eye contact

When we talk to other persons, we usually look at them for five to ten seconds before looking away. That is natural in one-to-one communication. The five second period sets your partners at ease whether you speak to one person or a large audience. If you look at them longer than five seconds it makes them feel *uncomfortable.* After ten seconds they normally feel *intimidated* or even *threatened.*

unbequem
eingeschüchtert
bedroht

Where to look

In a one-to-one situation try to keep a distance of four or five feet. Most people let their eyes wander around their listener's face, but there is one place we *tend to* rest. Find where your spot is – the right eye, *bridge of the nose,* left eye, or directly between the eyes? You may look at either a person's left eye or right eye. Any resting place near the eyes is acceptable. If you *feel uneasy* with a person that you are talking to in a job interview or a meeting with the boss, try looking at the person's *forehead.*

neigen zu
Nasenwurzel
sich unwohl fühlen
Stirn

Addressing a larger audience

To get into contact with your audience, you can't just look at them. *Survey* all your listeners before you start speaking. Your look must *convey* the feeling that you are trying to communicate with

überblicken
vermitteln

them. Concentrate intensively on each person you see for about five seconds. Make it *plain* to each person that you really want him or her to understand your *message*. Make each person feel that you are *delivering* the message for him or her alone. When you look at one person, dozens of people around that person will think you are talking just to them. Don't forget those at the far edges of the room or along your side of a conference table during meetings.

deutlich
Botschaft
senden

What you should not do

- Don't try to look directly in both eyes. It will make you and your opposite feel *embarrassed*.
- Don't look at your listener's *chest*, to the floor, over his shoulder etc.
- Don't keep your *eyelids* closed for up to two or three seconds. It conveys the message, "I really don't want to be here". Usually, your listeners won't want to be either.
- Don't *avoid* eye contact. The problem most of us have when we feel *pressure* is to *glance* at anything but our listener.
- Don't look *restlessly* in all directions like a *scared rabbit*. This conveys a nervousness that undermines our *credibility* and makes our listener uncomfortable.

peinlich berührt
Brust
Augenlider
vermeiden
Druck; blicken
unruhig
verängstigt; Kaninchen; Glaubwürdigkeit

Chapter 20

The farewell speech

Back at Ruver Georg Grosleger (**G**) is feeling out of sorts. He's had quite a few problems at the company. He meets Dr Koutert (**K**) Member of the Board. Georg feels that Koutert is a fair, direct fellow. They often play squash together. At an Indian restaurant:

G: Jesus, this curry is hot. I'm not used to this sort of thing.
K: It takes time. You get used to everything in time.
G: It's interesting that you say that. I've been here almost two years and I seem not to be getting accustomed to things, especially at the company … (*fade out*)
G: (*fade in*) … and so I've decided to give my notice.
K: I'm sorry about that. I …., well, I'll certainly talk to Dr Naston.

An interview that went wrong

A personnel manager found himself in an embarrassing situation. A month before, he had agreed to employ a new worker, but by the time the man arrived for his first day they had reorganised the company and the position he had intended to fill had disappeared. "Oh, don't worry," said the new employee, quite unconcerned. "The little bit of work I do won't be noticed by anybody."

⊛ Bye bye, Ruver ⊛

Back in the PR department. Georg, who has resigned, is making his farewell speech. This time there is no need to knock the table with a stapler. Everybody is attentive.

Ladies and Gentlemen of the Public Relations Department,
First of all let me thank you for coming together so late on a Friday afternoon. I know most of you are burning to get back to your families and goodness knows, you have little enough time with them. (*Calls from the audience*) Hear, hear!
As you will all probably know, I am here today to inform you of my resignation after almost two years in the company. You may ask yourselves why this should be, after all things are moving well. Ruver is steaming ahead at full power, jobs in our department are as safe as houses, as much as they can be in the private sector.
This is all good and different from when we first met. The chickens which were running around in those days all stride about now with purpose and people are achieving departmental as well as personal targets. For this support I thank you. My reasons for going were once summarised by a certain Englishman, Mr Ruskin, who said, "we have a certain work to do for our bread, and that is to be done strenuously; other work for our delight and that is to be done heartily; neither is to be done by halves or shifts."
So, Ladies and Gentlemen, this is a philosophy I also believe in. I have tried to do both things, to work for our living, our bread so to speak, and I hoped to work for some special enjoyment or psychological reward. It has become clear to me in the last six months or so that I have not succeeded in this second point. Therefore it is time to take my hat, to jump ship. No, my friends, this was an unfortunately chosen image. I'm not jumping ship, because the ship is not sinking, and there are certainly no rats aboard.
No, colleagues of PR, the vessel is strong and sea-worthy, capable of weathering the worst of our industrial storms. And our crew is pulling together. Well done, all of you!
I hope that when I have left you, impressions of what I have tried to do

here will not be all bad. I've heard it said by some people here that "Grosleger is a great man." It is well-known that this is a reference to my quite large shoe-size. But all joking apart I hope that you will consider that I have done my job as well as I consider you have done yours. Persistent, practical and patient, these have been the words to describe our progress during these two difficult years.
As for myself I would hope to find some sort of work which brings me fulfilment, in England I might add. In our period together I have grown fond of the English ways of going on with things. Of course, there have been ups and downs, we've lost our grip several times, but, please forgive me for taking the example of a foreigner, as Robert the Bruce said after watching the spider fall down time and again, "just like the spider, keep on trying, try, try again"! Or words to that effect. And that's what we have done.
I wish you all the best for the future, I'll do my best, too, and now let's drink a tiny drop of this bubbling liquid. To you, the best of luck!

Working with the language

Task 1: Key words in business

jobs in our department are	*die Arbeitsplätze sind in unserer Abteilung sicher*
inform someone of one's	*jemanden von seinem Ausscheiden informieren*
decide to give one's	*beschließen, seine Kündigung einzureichen*
.... from a	*von einem Posten zurücktreten*
work for one's	*für seinen Lebensunterhalt arbeiten*
.... together	*an einem Strang ziehen*
.... a storm	*einem Sturm standhalten*
.... difficult years	*Fortschritt während schwieriger Jahre*
work which brings	*Arbeit, die einen ausfüllt*
.... one's	*seine Ziele erreichen*

There have been .... and	*Es gab Höhen und Tiefen*
thank someone for his	*jemandem für seine Unterstützung danken*

Task 2: Thinker's corner

1. What reason does Georg give for his resignation?
2. Why does the author refer to "chickens running round"?
3. What is the major image here in this speech?

Task 3: Two ways of saying it

Can you find the second alternative?

1. I seem not to be getting *accustomed* to things at the company.
   I seem not to be getting .... to things at the company.
2. Let me thank you for *coming together* so late on a Friday afternoon.
   Let me thank you for .... here so late on a Friday afternoon.

Task 4: Say it the speaker's way

1. All are achieving departmental as well as personal *aims*.
2. My *motives* for going were once summarised by a certain Englishman, Mr Ruskin.
3. It has become *obvious* to me in the last six months that I have not *been successful* in this.

Task 5: Spot the mistake

1. I am here almost two years and I seem not to be getting accustomed to things at the company.
2. Ruver steams ahead at full power, things move well.
3. This is all good and different from when we first have met.

Ⓢ Spice up your speeches

Task 6: Rhetoric instead of straight questions

What did Georg say instead of

1. *Why should this be, after all things are moving?*
2. Now try two more alternatives using the verbs *wonder* and *want*.

Task 7: Say it with an image

Speakers often compare their company to a ship. It remains a cliché unless you can develop it in the course of your speech. Let's follow it through his speech. Your task is to complete the ship imagery.

Plain speech	Spicy speech
Ruver is doing extremely well.	Ruver *is* ....
I'm not abandoning the company.	I'm not ....
The company is in no trouble.	The ....
There are certainly no disloyal employees in the company.	There are certainly no ....
The company is in good shape.	The .... is ....
It is capable of surviving all the ups and downs in business.	It is capable of ....
And our staff works together as a team.	And our ....

Time for a smile

Call a meeting at 4.30 on Fridays
and you'll get little opposition.

Checkpoint: Complete checklists

Checklist 1: Preparing the speech

Before you start writing you should have a clear answer to these questions:

1. Why was I asked to deliver the speech?
2. What is the occasion?
3. How does the place and the hour of the speech affect its content?
4. What is the subject of my speech?
5. How long am I supposed to speak?
6. Who is going to be in the audience (their number and backgrounds)?
7. Are there any special circumstances I must take into account?
8. What is my purpose? What is my message? What are my arguments? Do I want to
   - inform?
   - entertain?
   - persuade?
9. How do I appeal to the audience? Shall I appeal to
   - logic?
   - emotions?
   - needs?
   - fears?
10. Which counter-arguments will I have to disarm?
11. How am I going to organise the parts of my speech?
    - chronologically
    - by cause and effect
    - with problem and solution
    - from weaker arguments to stronger arguments?
12. Do I have a good opening?
    - proverb
    - joke
    - anecdote
    - hot news

13. What is going into the body of my speech?
    - comparisons
    - contrasts
    - examples
    - facts
    - statistics
    - testimony by authorities
14. How can I conclude my speech?
15. Which media are best suited for my speech?
    - flipchart
    - OHP
    - slides
    - handouts
16. Is my outline clear enough to help me through my speech?

What not to say to the speaker

I'll never forget your speech – although I'll keep trying.

Checklist 2: Getting to know the audience

1. How can I find out more about my audience?
2. What are the education, background, functions of my listeners?
3. Is it a heterogeneous or homogeneous audience?
4. What age group do they belong to?
5. Will they need a coffee break?
6. Will it be an all male audience or will there be women, too?
7. What do they already know about my subject?
8. What do they expect of my speech?
9. Will they agree to what I have to say?
10. Will there be specialists among the listeners?
11. How can I compliment my audience?
12. Have I adapted the style of my speech to their background?
    - the length of my sentences?
    - the choice of my words?

- the figures of speech?
- the jokes?

13. Will they agree with me or will there be resistance?
14. Will there be a previous speaker talking about the same theme? Should I get in touch with him?

Time for a smile

"I wrote that speech myself", he told his boss.
"It's nice of you to take the blame," his boss replied.

Checklist 3: Rehearsing the speech

Use a mirror and a tape recorder.

1. Do I talk too low, too loud, too fast?
2. Where do I pause for effect?
3. How will I guide their attention?
4. Do I vary the tone of my voice?
5. Do I use body language?
   - facial expression
   - gestures
6. When do I need audio-visual support?

What not to say to the speaker

Anyone who told you to be yourself
couldn't have given you worse advice.

Checklist 4: Last minute preparations

Be on the set at least half an hour before the beginning.

1. Am I dressed for success?
2. Is the arrangement of chairs and tables adequate?
3. Have the handouts been distributed?
4. Can everybody see and hear me?

5. Can everybody see the flipchart and the screen for the OHP?
6. Do I need somebody to handle the audio-visual equipment?
7. Do I need a microphone? Does it work?
8. Does the OHP or the projector work properly?
9. Is the room well ventilated?

What not to say to the speaker

You talk so much I get hoarse just listening to you.

Scientists claim that the average person speaks 10,000 words a day. You're far above average.

Checklist 5: Watching the audience

Observe your audience, get feedback and adapt to their reactions.

1. Do they understand me?
2. Do I give them time to follow?
3. Do I speak freely?
4. Do I keep eye contact?
5. Do I bore them?
6. Shall I skip dry facts and figures?
7. Do they need a pause?
8. Do I keep to my outline?
9. Am I within the time limit?

What not to say to the speaker

Of course I'm listening to you; didn't you hear me yawning?

I've enjoyed listening to you. My mind needed a rest.

Well, Dear Reader, here ends Georg's episode at Ruver's. We're sure you all wish him success in his next project at ICE – he got the job, by the way. You can follow his career in *How to communicate effectively*, a book which helps you to shine in typical and critical business (and other) situations. See you!

Key to the tasks

1. The installation speech

Task 1: Key words in business

section leader
move *over* to another company
check somebody *out*
be *transferred* to Headquarters
on the *open* market
apply to a company
be well *recommended*
work *on* more of one's *own* initiative
in one's *capacity* as ...
support the Board of Management
somebody's tasks *include* among other things

Task 2: Thinker's corner

1. He's not a man for speeches but a man of action.
2. "As you all know I'm not a great man for speeches ..." Don't fish for compliments, don't make excuses, no false modesty. The audience will find out anyway. (Yes, it is a good one!)
3. It's a very difficult job to do, but Grosleger is the man for it and we must all support him.
4. He's sitting on the hot seat.
5. He is well recommended.
6. There may be bad feeling at the subsidiary that HQ just wants to dominate it with its own people.

Task 3: Three ways of saying it

1. I have great pleasure *in* introducing you *to* Mr G.
2. I have *the* great pleasure *of* introducing you *to* Mr G.
3. It's *my* pleasure *to* introduce Mr G.

Task 4: Say it the speaker's way

1. Could *I have your attention* for a minute?
2. To come to the reason *for our gathering here* ...

3. May I *present* Georg Grosleger from Germany?
4. This was in his *capacity* as an assistant.
5. *On behalf of* all of us, I'd like to wish you great success.

Task 5: Find the spices

Metaphor: Bavaria, the land of the leather trousers and the white sausage.

Irony: the centre of the world, Munich;
I have great pleasure in introducing you to the person who is to fill the gap – *if gap there will be* – after I've gone

Word play: Mr Grosleger is coming ... to sit on a hot *seat*. And all of us involved should try to ensure that it does not become an *ejector seat*.

Task 6: Watch out for repetition

The three repetitions are:

1. ... it is *not easy* to come to a foreign place to begin work.
2. We all know it is *a difficult time*, what with rationalisation, automation and globalisation.
3. It is a *difficult task*, but we believe that you are the right man to master it.

2. Waking up the staff

Task 1: Key words in business

be *on* a reconnaissance
call a meeting
talk *about* minor issues
work *to* rule
reach work targets
fulfil goals
achieve one's objectives
Jobs depend *on* it.
a description *of* functions
ask *for* co-operation
make a *contribution*

Task 2: Thinker's corner

1. We are at a crossroads.
2. a) Budgets are limited. b) They are not achieving targets because they are not working efficiently as a team.
3. May I now ask you for *comments, contributions and co-operation*? This is an alliteration. The three words begin with the same consonant 'c' (and the same vowel). The most important word is put at the end. This is another means of making an idea more memorable and giving the sentence an effective rhythm.
4. *Our* jobs depend on it. *Our* jobs are not guaranteed. We could be out.
5. B. He wants them to work as a team.

Task 3: Three ways of saying it

1. *Achieving* department *objectives* is vitally important
2. We have to *reach* our work *targets* efficiently.
3. These goals must *be fulfilled*.

Task 4: Say it the speaker's way

1. I *feel* that we need this meeting because we *are at a crossroads*.
2. I *want* each member of this department to *opt for* the second direction.
3. And when we don't do *our bit*, we could be out.
4. And he or she must be willing to *implement* what is necessary at full steam.
5. Then we'll *prioritise*. And finally *draw up* a time line.

Task 5: Say it with an image

1. We are running around like headless chickens (simile).
2. We're making one step forwards and two steps back (quotation).
3. Do what is necessary at full steam (image).
4. I'd like to see a colony of ants (metaphor).
5. Off to our ant-hill and let's just do it!
6. Let's spread our wings and fly with eagles.
7. Milestones have been kept to.

3. The keystone speech

Task 1: Key words in business

settle in a company
need someone's support
edit a speech
pull together
get one's work done
become the market leader
exchange of know-how
be *active* in the *field* of the automotive business

Task 2: Thinker's corner

1. What does Dr Mayer intend by addressing the workforce?
   C. To talk about past difficulties and present achievements.
2. What does he speak about in the fourth paragraph?
   He explains the function of the academy.
3. He makes his listeners see what is not yet there: On my left you see the entrance area open to the world, on my right, at the end of the academy, a showroom …
4. What does Dr Mayer say to lighten the atmosphere and bring things to a close? He ends with a quotation:
   "… if you stand up, you'll be seen. If you speak up, you'll be heard. If you sit down, you'll be appreciated."

Task 3: The structure of speeches

1. *First of all* I'd like to thank you for spending some of your valuable time to …
2. *And I want to add* a hearty "thank-you" to the men and women here.
3. *And now* to the reason for our being together today.
4. *And so I come to* the climax of our gathering here.
5. *And now to* finish.

Task 4: Say it the speaker's way

1. And so I come to the climax of *our gathering* here.
2. It is with great pleasure that I *cement this keystone into place.*
3. What is this academy *about*?
4. Ruver has had problems in the past, but it has *struggled through.*

Task 5: Find the spices

1. *pull* together in the Ruver *boat* to bring us *upstream* (metaphor)
2. the *rapids* of competition and rules and regulations (metaphor)
3. a *visiting card* for our activities in the field of the automotive industry (image)
4. *stones bound together* into an institution which is more than simply *brick and mortar* (imagery)
5. a *little giant*, a conservative company in the best meaning of the word, but progressive and flexible (paradox).

4. The Annual General Meeting

Task 1: Key words in business

promote to the Board
keep up the good work
proceed to the business of the meeting
mention a matter of personal interest
draw somebody's attention to
continue in one's capacity as head of development
give someone the *benefit* of one's experience
forecast business conditions in the coming year
the *supply* of raw materials is *undisturbed*

Task 2: Let money speak

net profits *amount* to …
represent an increase of … on the previous year
absorb an amount of …
propose a dividend of …
prices *remain* at their present level
profits will be *maintained*

prove a good investment
the volume of business has *risen* by 20 per cent.

Task 3: Thinker's corner

1. The speech is divided in three major parts:
   A. Personal matters B. Business matters C. Personnel matters
2. The themes of these sections:
   A. Personal matters
      1. Death of Mr Cardet
      2. Promotion of Dr Koutert
   B. Business matters
      1. Overview of last year's results
      2. Outlook for the future
   C. Personnel matters
      1. Changes of staff
      2. Working climate
3. The two different styles of speech Dr Naston uses:
   1. Formal style 2. Informative style, facts and figures
4. Stylistic feature:
      1. one idea is expressed by word pairs
      2. frequent use of adjectives
   Effect: Naston slows down the speed of his speech and gives the audience time to think; the word pairs in end position give rhythm to the speech.

Task 4: Polish up your English

1. I must remind you of the loss we have *sustained.*
2. I have two *matters of personal interest* to mention.
3. The other personal matter is *of a happier kind.*
4. It is our intention to continue this policy *as circumstances permit.*

Task 5: Find the spices

1. Dr Koutert has *climbed the weary path* to the Board (*metaphor*).
2. The *passing away of* Mr John Cardet (*euphemism*).
3. Modernisation *is still in the pipeline (image).*
4. Rumours that we will *streamline* the company are unfounded (*euphemism*).

Task 6: Say it the speaker's way

1. Mr John Cardet served us well in *good times and bad.*
2. We feel the loss of Mr Cardet's *wise counsel and shrewd foresight.*
3. And still more, we shall miss a *loyal and sincere friend.*
4. Dr Koutert will give us all the benefit of his considerable *experience and ability.*
5. We appreciate the *devotion and loyalty* of our staff.

5. The spontaneous speech

Task 1: Key words in business

request someone's help
the *annual* executive dinner
call on someone to do something
direct a speech *towards* someone
spend one's working life in the *service* of one company
have a *stake* in the company
out of *office* hours
work *for* one's *living*
run a company

Task 2: Thinker's corner

1. Bryan creates a light, positive atmosphere in the early part of the speech by using a humorous quotation.
2. "I'm not one of those rare birds who live for their work."
3. "Now I ask you, why should I spend ....?" The rhetorical question involves the audience. They compare their answer to the speaker's. It also brings the speaker closer to his listeners.
4. He announces the end of his speech by using irony at the expense of his own person. "But I feel that my time has elapsed, so I will end by closing in a way you'll all like – by closing my mouth!"

Task 3: Polite noises for speakers

1. I can say in all *sincerity* that I am very pleased to have the *honour* of proposing the toast to the Company.

2. But the fact that makes it such an easy and, indeed, *pleasurable* a *task* is simply that it is out of office hours.
3. I'm not going to *pretend* that I'm one of those *rare* birds who live for their work.
4. I ask you to *join* me in drinking to the Company's continued *prosperity*.

Task 4: Create your own toasts

1. *Erheben wir unsere Gläser und trinken auf die Zukunft unserer Firma.*	Let's *raise* our glasses to the *future* of our company.
2. *Ich erhebe mich, um auf das Wohl unserer Gäste unserer Firma zu trinken.*	I *rise* to *toast* the guests of our company.
3. *Ich schlage vor, wir trinken auf den Abschluß unseres Vertrags.*	I'd like to *propose / suggest* a *toast* to the *conclusion* of our contract.
4. *Ich möchte einen Toast auf die Firma ausbringen.*	I'd like to *suggest / propose* a *toast* to the company.
5. *Feiern wir unsere Vereinbarung mit einem Glas Champagner.*	Let's *celebrate* our *agreement* with a glass of champagne.

Task 5: Find the spices

1. Zeugma:
   But I see that my time has elapsed, so I will end by *closing in a way you'll all like – by closing my mouth!* (close a speech and one's mouth)
2. Irony:
   I expect to be here another twenty years – *I thank you for accepting that threat.*
3. Freudian slip:
   Bryan resumes the opening quotation and changes it (lean away). I should say I'd rather climb a *g... ehmm ... a wall that is leaning away from me or ....* He leaves it to the listeners to complete the sentence.

4. Anaphora (parallelism) and climax:
   I like the atmosphere, I like my colleagues, and – believe it or not – I even like our superiors. The parallelisms start with the least important and end with the most important idea.

6. A pep talk

Task 1: Key words in business

talk *shop*
take the *helm*
work *within* the *framework* of the team
no *substitute for* teamwork
have a *stake in* the company
work *for* the *common* good
efficiency *at* a high *level*
enlarge the restaurant.
stimulate motivation
restructure the bonus scheme
depend on the co-operation
suggestions for *raising* efficiency

Task 2: Thinker's corner

1. The keynote of the introduction: motivating the staff.
2. The key word which summarises the main theme of the speech: co-operation / teamwork.
3. He compares the team to a game of cricket where you must play both individually and as a whole team.

Task 3: Say it the speaker's way

1. I'll have to do it *without preparation*.	I'll have to do it *off the cuff*.
2. We all have *an interest* in the company.	We all have *a stake* in the company.
3. I'll take *control* in this matter.	I'll take *the helm* in this matter.
4. *In the name* of Ruver, I thank you.	*On behalf* of Ruver, I thank you.

Task 4: Highlight your verbs

1. Success *does depend* primarily on co-operation.
2. The same *is* true for our company. (No, because auxiliary *to be*)
3. Each member of the team does *have* his own job to do. (have is not an auxiliary here)
4. He *did want* to stimulate your motivation.
5. You *may* be pleased to hear that the restaurant *will* be enlarged. (No, because auxiliary *to be*)

Task 5: Discover the spices

1. Metaphors to create a "we"-feeling.
   A. We all have *a stake* in the company.
   (stake means 1. money, etc risked or gambled on the unknown result of a race or a card-game; 2. money, etc invested in an enterprise, giving you an interest or a share in it).
   B. I hope you will always think of *this ship not* as "it", but as "us".
2. He used an image drawn from the field of games to criticise individualism and selfishness.
   Our activities are too complicated to allow us to *play musical chairs*.

7. Speaking to convince

Task 1: Keywords in business

adapt a range to use diesel
present a case to the Board
think of the cost *involved*
put one's money *on* petrol
support and complement each other
reduce pollution
raise arguments against …
summarise the *gist* of the diesel's advantages
be *at* the state of the *art*
be *involved* in the development of engines
a question of *performance*
technology has been *upgraded*

Task 2: Thinker's corner

1. What is the effect of *"I'm not against them (petrol engines). Quite the opposite, in fact"*.
   He anticipates *any* opposition to his idea, creates a feeling of complement rather than alternatives. He disarms possible arguments.
2. *The press* is an abstract generalisation. The speaker splits it into the concrete individual elements to create diversity and to stress the idea of 'everywhere'.
3. Again *people* or *everybody* is a generalisation. The individual representatives create a more vivid impression. In both cases using several words to express the same thing emphasises the idea, makes it more dramatic and gives the audience time to digest it.

Task 3: Four ways of saying it

However, I can verify that the modern diesel engine emits
far less pollution in its exhaust than its petrol-driven sister.
☐ 'and' would change the meaning

Task 4: Three ways of saying 'thank you'

1. I gratefully accept
2. I am deeply grateful to you for
3. Let me express my gratitude for

} the opportunity of being able to speak to you here

Task 5: Say it the speaker's way

	What he meant ...	**and how he put it.**
1.	Let's hear what you have to say.	The *floor* is *yours*.
2.	I won't waste your time.	I'd like to come *straight* to the *point*.
3.	I have nothing more to say.	I've *taken* enough of your *time*.

Task 6: How to introduce a speaker

1. I have the great pleasure of *introducing* Mr X.
   Es ist mir eine große Freude, Ihnen Herrn X vorstellen zu dürfen.
2. We have the honour of *being* addressed by Professor X on the theme of pollution.

Wir haben die Ehre, Professor X zum Thema Umweltbelastung zu hören.

3. Mr X, will now *speak* to you about the problem of ...
   Herr X wird nun zu Ihnen über das Problem ... sprechen.
4. We're all *looking* forward to your presentation.
   Wir freuen uns alle auf Ihre Präsentation.
5. Mr X, we're very *interested* to hear your *point* of view.
   Herr X, es interessiert uns sehr, Ihre Meinung zu hören.

Task 7: Discover the spices

1. Petrol and diesel cannot walk 'hand in hand'. This is a personification to emphasise that diesel and petrol engines won't be rivals.
2. *To be a lasting part of all our futures* is an ellipsis. The complete sentence would be: We need both technologies *to be a lasting part of all our futures.* It reduces the sentence to a slogan or key phrase in order to draw the attention to the message.
3. It is what we call a particularisation. Filsinger wants to stress that the diesel would reach a wider clientèle, not just the young and rich.
4. Again a personification to repeat the fact that the petrol and the diesel engine won't be in competition.

8. Singing a person's praises

Task 1: Key words in business

parcel something up
be *responsible* for a product *range*
consider reducing a budget
a product *sells* well
eliminate a budget for a range
accept a *decision*
commit oneself to completing a project
design products optimally
place a *priority* on teamwork
for the *benefit* of our commercial interests
achieve the *optimum* from a team

Task 2: Thinker's corner

1. What is the effect of the anecdote in the introduction?
   It shows the human side of an employee, it gives all the staff something to associate with, it lightens the atmosphere for the speech.
2. What would you say is the main idea of this speech?
   B. to emphasise teamwork

Task 3: How many ways of saying it?

A: *Although* he was new to the company
B: he was able to grab the bull by the horns
2. also

Task 4: Wordbuilder's corner

ability	*able*	fähig
commitment	*committed*	engagiert
creativity	*creative*	schöpferisch
dedication	*dedicated*	pflichtbewußt
determination	*determined*	entschlossen
discipline	*disciplined*	diszipliniert
efficiency	*efficient*	tüchtig
honesty	*honest*	ehrlich
ingenuity	*ingenious*	erfinderisch, genial
loyalty	*loyal*	treu
reliability	*reliable*	zuverlässig
strictness	*strict*	streng

If business people …

have success	they are *successful*
have a clear mind	they are *clear-minded*
work hard	they are *hardworking*
help others	they are *helpful*
know a lot	they are *knowledgeable*

Task 5: Find the spices

1. Climax: And all this to achieve the optimum from himself, from his team, for the benefit of the company.

2. Repetition: And I believe his *motivation, dedication and determination* are a lesson for all of us.
3. Climax: Mr Koutert has been *the new boy, a project leader, a department leader, head of research and a Member of the Board*.
4. Hyperbole: In that project he had more than *two hundred percent* success, a trend which has continued.

9. The mission statement

Task 1: Key words in business

everything under one *umbrella*
be a *leading* player in a *field*
cover the needs of the driver
build a lasting *relationship* with the customer
further develop a beneficial link with the suppliers
adapt to customers' needs
aim to *offer* the customers perfect products
offer *enhanced* quality for the customer
give *advice* to the customer's *benefit*
be in a *state* of permanent *change*
perfect the business *processes*

Task 2: Thinker's corner

1. Because the target group uses the Internet. They need brief information when they click around.
2. It emphasises the positive result of these actions. It moves the reader towards a feeling of overall improvement and efficiency.
3. It is general. The writer does not want to go into technical details or advertising slogans etc. He wishes to state targets to be set and achieved with and for the customers.

Task 3: Five ways of saying it

1. We *aim* to develop alongside those who produce our parts to raise quality.
2. Our *ambition* has always been to offer our customers perfect products.
3. *Our aim* is to draw these three threads together into a powerful cord.
4. *Our intention* is to further develop a link with all our suppliers.
5. Your heart's content is our *intent*.

Task 4: Highlighting your ideas

Type 1:
1. I *do want* to stimulate your motivation.
2. We don't have many cars, but what we *do have* are all winners.
3. And they *do cover* the needs of the driver.

Type 2:
1. *It has always been* our ambition to offer our customers perfect products.
2. *It is our aim/objective/goal to* draw these three threads of business practice together into a powerful cord.
3. *It is our intention/aim/objective/goal* to further develop a link with all our suppliers.

Task 5: Say it the speaker's way

1. We *don't have many* cars in this off-road world, but what we do have are all winners.
2. We *do not have the worst* relationship to our suppliers.
3. We are *not the largest* company.

Task 6: Find the spices

1. Trias	Whatever range you choose, you will meet *power, reliability, and innovation.*
2. Trias 3. Extended metaphor	Suppliers, staff and customers – it is our aim to *draw* these three *threads* of business practice *together into a powerful cord* in which everyone can trust.

10. Toast to the staff

Task 1: Thinker's corner

1. Can you give an example of irony in the speech?
   … there is no reason why even the dirty job of making money …..
2. How is Mr. Patten complemented in the last paragraph of this toast?
   … old in service, but young in spirit …
3. What is the main purpose of Dr Koutert's speech to his staff?
   To foster teamwork and loyalty.

Task 2: Thinker's corner

1. Why does Tom Disney begin with his excuses in the first paragraph? He wants to protect himself from not doing well later because he hasn't had time to prepare the toast.
2. In the second paragraph there is a joke. Explain.
   He jokes that the staff is so motivated that they don't wish to leave, or can't be fired because of their contracts.
3. What is the main image in the speech?
   The idea that in some way the company and the atmosphere is like that of a family.

Task 3: Three ways of saying it

make *hold* *deliver*	} a speech	make *propose* *suggest*	} a toast

11. Awarding an award

Task 1: Key words in business

witness a presentation	*attend* a presentation
sponsor an event	*promote* an event
donate a trophy	*offer* a trophy
award a prize to the winner	*give* a prize to the winner
undergo an examination	*sit for* an examination
be *noted* for one's results	be *distinguished* for one's results

extend a hearty thank-you to somebody	*say* a hearty thank-you to somebody
abandon the family enterprise	*give up* the family enterprise

Task 2: Let's go woggling again

Annette has *merited* the award for both a new ingenious technical *breakthrough* and for her *contribution* to the welfare of your community. Annette Sauter has further *developed* her FBA-99 into a small and light multi-*purpose* baking *device* which can *process* not only bread but also Battlemoore's fine pottery, for which your town is well-*known* far beyond the boundaries of this county.

Task 3: Build your vote of thanks

I should like to *express* my thanks to the *panel* of judges, to the Battlemoore Chamber of Commerce which has *created* the award and in particular to you, Mr Reckless, for your kind words and to your company who *has* so generously *sponsored* this event.
I'm very honoured and *proud* to have been *chosen* to receive the Roosting Award, which is one of the most highly *regarded* awards made in our part of the world. I *will keep* the trophy on my desk at IBM, where I hope it will *inspire* me to *imitate* the success of *previous* winners. Expansion plans for IBM are already under way, and I hope to be *opening* a second small factory near Battlemoore in the next few months, *providing* more jobs and *wealth* for this beloved town.

12. Speech to a retiring colleague

Task 1: Key words in business

take early *retirement*
a *well-deserved* retirement
retire after thirty years' continuous *service*
no one is *indispensable*
it is difficult to *do without* him
scowl at the junior *clerks*
treat everybody with *courtesy*

Task 2: Thinker's corner

1. Dr Naston mentions that they will miss Tom Stow five times.
2. Dr Naston includes Dr Stow's humanity, cheerfulness and natural friendliness.
3. Dr Stow's many sides: "To some he has been one of those bosses, to be addressed as "Sir". Others have known him just as Dr Stow. To others again, he has been simply "Stow".
4. Dr Naston doesn't refer to any of Stow's business skills and achievements for the company.

Task 3: Dropping themes

1. I'm not going to touch upon … 2. I do not want to bore you with details about 3. It is not so important to mention 4. I will not waste your time with 5. I am not going to deal with	} the numerous patents he filed for the company.

Task 4: Guided translation

1. *Our sincere* wishes for your *happiness and health* accompany you.
2. I'm sure *I speak for all us* when I wish you a *pleasant* and satisfying eve of life.
3. From the bottom of our *hearts* we'd like to wish you *all the best* for the next *stage* in life.
4. You know you take our *best wishes* for a happy and *successful future* with you.

Task 5: Do you remember Dr Naston's feelings?

1. It is with a *sense* of real *loss* that we see him go.
2. We shall be *reminded* of him for a long time to *come*.
3. We cannot *pretend* that we are happy to see him *leave* us.
4. On an *occasion* such as this our feelings are *bound* to be *mixed*.
5. We going to *miss* a man who has *brought* much *humanity* with him.

13. A vote of thanks

Task 1: Key words in business

intend to retire
the hum of the market
a *cog* in the machine
receive loyal co-operation from ...
the *achievements* of a team
research in the archives
apply for a patent
complaints of the staff

Task 2: Thinker's corner

1. I shall find it difficult to live without the constant complaints of the staff.
   I appreciate that you have chosen as a present my very first flop, the first patent I ever applied for at this company: the Ruvlet 200 gear transmission. What more could I want to accompany me in the twilight of my days.
2. A cog is a small part in a large impersonal system. Also the image has become a cliché. Clichés shouldn't be used too often.
3. Dr Stow's main approach in his reply to the toast is to make it clear that the team is important, and to praise the other members.
4. A difficult question to answer. The imagery is drawn from cricket, a sport no German will understand. It means: Now my turn to play, my turn to work has passed, and I shall watch from a distance.

Task 3: Spot the mistakes ...

1. It is to my garden that I intend to retire – I *did* not say rest!
2. It is difficult for me to realise that today I *am leaving* this firm.
3. I have no doubt that the company *will* get along pretty well without me.
4. I was going to say that I *have* only *been* a cog in the machine.
5. I *think* a happier and more accurate description would be a member of a team.

Task 4: Odd man out

1. It is difficult for me to realise that today I am leaving this firm where I have worked for so many years.
   Here "it is ..." is not used for emphasis.

Task 5: Modify your statements

1. I shall, I think, be *quite* happy without my work.
2. I have not the slightest doubt that the company will get along *pretty* well without me.
3. And it is the thought of leaving this team that makes parting *rather* difficult for me.

Task 6: Test your synonyms

1. I shall always *prize* this gift and what it stands for.
   ☐ value
2. I have been only a *cog* in the machine ... .
   ☐ part
3. The small *part* I have played in this team has been made easy for me.
   ☐ role
4. Thank you for your kind *offering* and especially for the kind wishes that have come with it.
   ☐ gift
5. I have no *doubt* that the company will get along pretty well without me.
   ☐ uncertainty

14. What to say at weddings

Task 1: Key words in business

get down to business
land a contract
be *acquainted* with a matter
give someone a good *run for* his money
jump into the *deep end*
be *instrumental in* doing something

Task 2: Thinker's corner

1. He used the extended image of various sports, squash, fishing, swimming (*jumping in the deep end*).
2. God is paraphrased as "the Great Spirit in the heavens", Carol as "this young creature."
3. She means "We decided to take the risk." See also *Spice up your Speeches*.

Task 3: How to refer to the occasion

1. You all know the *reason* for our little *get-together*.
2. And a very pleasant *occasion* it is, too.
3. I'd like to take this *opportunity* to wish them luck from the bottom of my heart.

Task 4: How to characterise the occasion

1. Promotion, wedding:	this *pleasant* occasion
2. Inauguration, ribbon cutting:	this *solemn* occasion
3. Funeral, death:	this *sad* occasion

Task 5: Find the spices

1. On one occasion we were having a *tiny drop of something a bit stronger.*
2. There was *this young creature*, a real charmer, playing at a good level.
3. *I don't have a crystal ball*, none of us *do*, except of course, *the great spirit in the heavens*.

15. The product launch

Task 1: Key words in business

launch a product
the *top* of the *range*
play a *major part* in
the *latest* technological *achievement*
get *down* to *brass* tacks

the *features* of a product
poll potential clients
the Overlander is *targeted* at all markets
offer the customer reliable *after-sales*
a *hallmark* of technology
the car is as safe as *houses*
safety is *vital*
hit the target
an *ambitious* project
these are *mere teething* problems

Task 2: Thinker's corner

1. Like a horse the Overlander can get into places where an ordinary car can't; also because it is very powerful.
2. How often does the speaker use animal images? Six times.
3. He concentrates the listeners' attention to the car by communicating directly with the listeners and by involving them. (Allow yourselves a few minutes … to cast your eyes over fine horse of a car as it conquers terrestrial opponents. Please take your time to appreciate its elegance.)
4. Which image is used to show that there are always problems in the beginning phase of a project? "… there were teething problems …"

Task 3: Guiding the listeners' attention

1. Please *take* your time to appreciate its elegance.
2. *Allow* yourselves a few minutes, Honoured Visitors, to cast your eyes over this fine horse of a car.
3. And now, if I could *have* your *attention*, a few historical facts.

Task 4: How to structure your speech

1. We *are gathered* here to celebrate our latest *achievement*.
2. I'*ll describe* what I'*m going to talk* about.
3. I'*ll give* you a *brief* history of the product.
4. I'*ll go* from the general *down to* the detail.
5. And there are many other things. We'*ll go into* all that *later*.

Task 5: How to be brief

1. My first comment is that I'm going to *keep* it *short*.
2. To *put* it in a *nutshell*, the Overlander is targeted at all markets.
3. Our best brains were called up for service, engineering, marketing, sales, customer service, to *mention* just a *few*.

16. Motivating the workforce

Task 1: Key words in business

go *public*.
stand to the workers
support the trade union
an argument *holds water*
rationalise *workplaces away*
release a *statement* to the press
reaction to *intended dismissals*
What *action* shall we *take*?

call *for* a strike	*einen Streik ausrufen*
put *in* hours of work	*Arbeitszeit aufbringen*
stand *up for* one's rights	*für seine Rechte einstehen*
come *out on* a wild cat strike	*in einen wilden Streik treten*

Task 2: Thinker's corner

1. If you had to find one theme to characterise this speech what would it be?
   B. Let's negotiate
   C. Let's go public
2. From which thematic field does the speaker take most of her images?
   C. From war
3. What is the trade union official's main intention?
   A. appeal to logic

Task 3: Beef up your word power

adjective	**noun**	**noun**
loyal	*loyalty*	Treue
decisive	*decisiveness*	Entschlossenheit
public	*public*	Öffentlichkeit
verb	**noun**	
dismiss	*dismissal*	Entlassung
intend	*intention*	Absicht
expect	*expectation*	Erwartung

Task 4: Fit in the spices

What she might have said	**... what she actually said**
Let's face the problem.	Let's *look* the problem squarely in the eye.
I'll come straight to the point.	I won't *beat* about the *bush*.
Let's try to find common ground with the management.	Let's build *bridges* to the management.
Let's keep our eyes open and act carefully.	Let's keep our *powder* dry.
Let's go to the press.	Let's go *public*.
Take your places and help to defend our cause.	Once more into the *breach*.
Support the cause of the trade union	Follow the *banner* of the trade union.
Attack somebody unexpectedly	Pull the *carpet* from under somebody's *feet*.

17. Presenting your thing

Task 1: Key words for presenters

make a presentation to *executives*
receive the pre-presentation documentation
refer to the handouts
switch on the OHP
explain with the help of a flipchart

come up with an interesting invention
be in contact with an inventor
take notes
make it *as brief as* possible

Task 2: Thinker's corner

1. The Professor appeals to fears about one's health and to stress.
   Totally frustrated you phone the police.
   An escape from all this stress.
   You can't drive off to your next vital appointment.
   High blood pressure.
   Think of your health.
2. What are the three main steps of the presentation?
   1. The professor describes the problem.
   2. He shows what the consequences are.
   3. He offers a solution.
3. He uses several different direct forms of address: *Ladies and Gentlemen, Dear Listeners, Honourable Spectators, Fellow Sufferers.*

Task 3: Preposition exercise

1. You are acquainted *with* the reputation *of* the inventor.
2. I ask you to bear *with* me and be patient.
3. I acknowledge that I'm sadly *out of* practice.
4. What, you may ask, do the letters stand *for*?
5. I'm talking *about* the Personal Parking Protector.

Task 4: Guiding the attention of the audience

1. Please *turn* your attentions to the upper part of the flipchart.
2. *Cast* your eyes over sheet two.
3. Just *refer* to the handouts in front of you.
4. Please *observe* that the bumper bar B is movable.
5. *There* you *have* it!

Task 5: More ways of beginning your speech

1. May I say at the *outset* that …
2. Let's *start*/*begin* with …
3. I'll *start* off by dealing with …

Task 6: Say it the speaker's way

1. You are *acquainted* with the reputation of the inventor.
2. I ask you to *bear* with me and be patient.
3. I *acknowledge* that I'm sadly out of practice.
4. What, you may ask, do the letters P.P.P. *stand for*?

18. The after-dinner speech

Task 1: Key words in business

attend a dinner
complaints about quality
complement the dinner with an after-dinner speech
come up with a *range* of good results.
a day of *trouble-shooting*
solve a problem
have *different priorities*

Task 2: Thinker's corner

1. He keeps the atmosphere light by referring to non-business things, e.g. the food, alcohol, the car as a concept, not a product.
2. Dr Koutert avoids jokes and humour because this is an international meeting. European humour is often not understood by Asians.
3. Why does he not tell any stories or anecdotes? It's a more formal meeting. One reason might be that stories or anecdotes would fail to create common ground because they are too personal.

Task 3: Spot the mistake

1. We all *have* our ideas. Have (*haben, besitzen*) is not used in the progressive (*Verlaufsform*).
2. The past two years *have been*, well, not the easiest to manoeuvre. (The *past two years* are not over yet, therefore present perfect.)
3. What *was* it (the car) in the past, what is it now, and what will it look like in the future? (The car *of the past,* is no longer produced today. It belongs to the past, therefore past tense.)
4. But as I look around me … a thought *crosses* my mind. (A thought is too fast to cross your mind in the progressive.)

5. I am aware today *was* a day of trouble-shooting. Dr Koutert uses the past to refer to unpleasant things in the past. He does not want to link trouble-shootings and problems with the present.

Task 4: Adding some spices

1. Let's leave these worldly pleasures for a moment.
2. The market at present is like *a raging storm*.
3. And we want to remain *sea-worthy*.
4. This year we *bought* some companies and some *bad headaches*.

19. Interview for a new job

Task 1: Key words in business

read someone's CV
rethink one's strategy
land a good job
need new *challenges*
get a job as an *assistant* to the *Board*
take over a department at Ruver
apply for a position
in the *field* of public relations
lose one's job
change to another company

Task 2: Say it the speaker's way

Deep down in my heart I feel I need new challenges	*In my heart of hearts* I feel I need new challenges.
This position *suits me better*.	This position *is more up my street*.
It could give me a chance to get back to *my professional origins*.	It could give me a chance to get back *to the roots*.
Quite honestly, the answer is yes.	*To tell you the truth*, the answer is yes.
It doesn't make any difference to me.	*That's all the same* to me.
I *got* a good job and a *problem*.	I *landed* a good job and a *stomach ache*.

Task 3: Two ways of saying it

I took *a shot at* it.	I *went for* it.
To come back to your question	*To return* to your question
It's a chance to *create* advertising	It's a chance to *build up* advertising

Task 4: Did you get the message?

1. The *gist of it* is that I need success.
   B. the most important reason
2. The problem was the *red-tape*.
   C. excessive bureaucracy
3. But *actually*, I'd like to ask you to give me some information about yourself.
   A. as a matter of fact
4. It could give me a chance to get *back to the roots*.
   B. back to what I have been trained for

20. The farewell speech

Task 1: Key words in business

jobs in our department are *safe*
inform someone of one's *resignation*
decide to give one's *notice*
resign from a *post*
work for one's *living*
pull together
weather a storm
progress during difficult years
work which brings *fulfilment*
achieve one's *targets*
There have been *ups* and *downs*.
thank someone for his *support*

Task 2: Thinker's corner

1. What reason does Georg give for his resignation? His work has not brought the fulfilment he had expected and hoped for.

2. Why does the author refer to "chickens running round"? It is a reference back to his initial speech to his department. Two years before they had run around without direction. Now the department works efficiently.
3. What is the major image here in this speech? The company is like a steamer or a ship.

Task 3: Two ways of saying it

1. I seem not to be getting *accustomed* to things at the company.
   I seem not to be getting *used* to things at the company.
2. Let me thank you for *coming together* so late on a Friday afternoon.
   Let me thank you for *gathering* here so late on a Friday afternoon.

Task 4: Say it the speaker's way

1. All are achieving departmental as well as personal *targets*.
2. My *reasons* for going were once summarised by a certain Englishman, Mr Ruskin.
3. It has become *clear* to me in the last six months that I have not *succeeded* in this.

Task 5: Spot the mistake

1. I'*ve been here* almost two years and I seem not to be getting accustomed to things at the company.
2. Ruver *is steaming* ahead at full power, things *are moving* well.
3. This is all good and different from when we first *met*.

Task 6: Rhetoric instead of a straight question

1. *You may ask yourselves* why this should be, after all things are moving well.
2. *You may wonder* why this should be, after all things are moving well.
   You may want to know why this should be, after all things are moving well.

Task 7: Say it with an image

Plain speech	Spicy speech
Ruver is doing extremely well.	Ruver *is steaming ahead at full power.*
I'm not abandoning the company.	I'm not *jumping ship.*
The company is in no trouble.	The *ship is not sinking*.
There are certainly no disloyal employees in the company.	There are certainly no *rats aboard*.
The company is in good shape.	The *vessel* is *sea-worthy*.
It is capable to survive all the ups and downs in business.	It is capable of *weathering the worst of our industrial storms.*
And our staff works together as a team.	And our *crew is pulling together.*

Interesting Phrases

as they appear in the chapters

be careful with …	*vorsichtig sein mit …*
that may be, but …	*das mag sein, aber …*
I'm sorry to say it but …	*es tut mir leid, aber …*
That brings me to another point.	*Das bringt mich auf einen anderen Punkt zu sprechen.*
Let it go at that.	*Lassen wir es dabei.*
Let's go for it!	*Packen wir's an!*
Could I have your attention?	*Darf ich um Ihre Aufmerksamkeit bitten?*
I'm not a great man for speeches.	*Ich bin kein Mann großer Worte.*
And to come to the reason for …:	*Und um auf den Grund für … zu kommen:*
I have great pleasure in …	*Es ist mir ein großes Vergnügen …*
I'm sure you can count on …	*Ich bin mir sicher, Sie können auf … zählen*
To keep it short …	*Um es kurz zu fassen …*
On behalf of …	*Im Namen von …*
We're pulling together.	*Wir ziehen am gleichen Strang.*
work to rule	*nach Vorschrift arbeiten*
It'll take care of itself.	*Es regelt sich von allein.*
I've got the message.	*Ich hab's kapiert.*
We're at a crossroads.	*Wir sind am Scheideweg.*
keep within the budget	*das Budget einhalten*
do it at full steam	*mit Volldampf drangehen*
run around like headless chicken	*wie aufgescheuchte Hühner herumlaufen*
one step forwards, two steps back	*ein Schritt vorwärts, zwei zurück*
I want to keep it short.	*Ich möchte mich kurz fassen.*
or to put it in another way	*anders gesagt/mit anderen Worten*
own up to something	*etwas zugeben*
How are you settling in?	*Wie haben Sie sich eingewöhnt?*
I have full confidence in you.	*Ich vertraue Ihnen voll und ganz.*
I'd like to start by …	*Zuallererst möchte ich aber …*
I'd like to add a hearty thank-you to …	*Mein herzlicher Dank gilt …*
We have struggled through.	*Wir haben uns durchgekämpft.*
And, if I may mention it …	*Und wenn ich das noch erwähnen dürfte …*

With this act I wish …	*Und damit möchte ich …*
Keep in mind that …	*Bedenken Sie, daß …*
Keep up the good work!	*Machen Sie weiter so!*
He's climbed the path to …	*Er ist zum … aufgestiegen.*
We've given a lot of thought to …	*Wir haben uns viele Gedanken über … gemacht.*
Let's stride forward together.	*Laßt uns den Weg gemeinsam beschreiten.*
I can say in all sincerity that …	*Ich kann ohne Bedenken sagen, daß …*
I have the honour of …	*Es ist mir eine Ehre, zu …*
I'm not going to pretend that …	*Ich will nicht so tun, als ob …*
I should take the helm.	*Ich sollte das Ruder übernehmen.*
I'm honoured to reply.	*Es ist mir eine Ehre, darauf zu antworten.*
The floor is yours.	*Sie haben das Wort.*
Let me express my gratitude.	*Erlauben Sie mir, meine tiefste Dankbarkeit zum Ausdruck zu bringen.*
Straight to the point.	*Um gleich zur Sache zu kommen.*
We have to put our money on …	*Wir müssen auf … setzen.*
Don't get me wrong!	*Verstehen Sie mich nicht falsch!*
Here are some hard facts: …	*Ein paar harte Fakten: …*
I've taken enough of your time.	*Ich habe genug von Ihrer Zeit in Anspruch genommen.*
sing a person's praises	*jemanden loben*
parcel something up	*einpacken*
We are proud to be …	*Wir sind stolz darauf …*
It's our ambition to …	*Es ist unser Ehrgeiz, zu …*
row in the same direction	*das gleiche Ziel verfolgen*
the first link in the chain	*das erste Glied in der Kette*
draw the threads together	*die Fäden zusammenführen*
Let me just say this!	*Ich möchte nur noch eins sagen!*
I have no doubt whatsoever that …	*Ich habe keinerlei Zweifel, daß …*
make it short and sweet	*sich kurz fassen*
It's my privilege and pleasure to …	*Es ist mir eine Ehre und ein Vergnügen, zu …*
My heart goes out to anybody who …	*Mein tiefstes Mitgefühl gilt all jenen, die …*
I'm not on top of things at the moment.	*Ich habe im Augenblick nicht alle Informationen darüber.*

Let out all the stops!	*Mit Volldampf voraus!*
On an occasion such as this …	*Bei einem Anlaß wie diesem …*
be a cog in a machine	*ein Rädchen im Getriebe sein*
still, all joking aside	*Spaß beiseite*
My innings has come to an end.	*Meine Zeit ist abgelaufen.*
It put me in mind of …	Es hat mich an … erinnert.
Cast your minds back to …	*Versetzen Sie sich in Gedanken zurück zu …*
get down to business	*zur Sache kommen*
land the fish / the big one	*einen dicken Fisch an Land ziehen*
jump in the deep end	*ins Ungewisse springen*
The speech went down badly.	*Die Rede ist nicht gut angekommen.*
launch a range	*Produktionsreihe auf den Markt bringen*
Allow yourselves a few minutes to …	*Nehmen Sie sich ein paar Minuten, um zu …*
hit the target	*ins Schwarze treffen*
have teething problems	*Anlaufprobleme haben*
put it in a nutshell	*kurz gesagt*
it's a hallmark …	*es ist ein Markenzeichen*
It's as safe as houses.	*Es ist so sicher wie die Bank von England.*
say a few words of praise	*ein paar Worte des Lobes sagen*
I won't beat about the bush.	*Ich werde nicht um den heißen Brei herumreden.*
We won't take it lying down.	*Wir geben uns nicht so einfach geschlagen.*
stand up for one's rights	*für seine Rechte eintreten*
come out on a wild-cat strike	*in einen wilden Streik treten*
look the problem squarely in the eye	*dem Problem gerade ins Auge sehen*
follow the banner	*loyal sein*
May I say at the outset …	*Einleitend möchte ich sagen, daß …*
Please, bear with me.	*Bitte, haben Sie etwas Geduld mit mir.*
Let me come straightaway to …	*Lassen Sie mich direkt zu … kommen.*
Please refer to the handouts.	*Bitte, nehmen Sie die Tischvorlage zur Hand.*
do the honours	*etwas übernehmen*
to round off this fine dinner	*um dieses nette Abendessen abzurunden*

It's a joy for me to …	*Es ist mir eine Freude, zu …*
A thought crossed my mind.	*Da kam mir ein Gedanke.*
remain sea-worthy	*seetauglich bleiben*
come full circle	*den Kreis schließen*
set one's mind on something	*sich auf etwas versteifen*
the gist of it is that …	*der Kern der Sache ist, daß …*
In my heart of hearts …	*In meinem tiefsten Inneren …*
land a good job	*eine gute Stelle ergattern*
red tape	*Bürokratie*
It is right up my street.	*Es liegt ganz auf meiner Wellenlänge.*
take a shot at something	*etwas versuchen*
Ruver is streaming ahead at full power.	*Ruver gibt Vollgas.*
jump ship	*das sinkende Schiff verlassen*
weather the storm	*die Talsohle überstehen*
There have been ups and downs	*es gab gute und schlechte Zeiten*
to lose one's grip	*den Halt verlieren*
to kick someone's arse (AM slang)	*in den Hintern treten*
You're not making it easy on us.	*Du machst es uns nicht einfach.*

Word aid

A

abandon the company
die Firma verlassen
abolish
abschaffen
above
über
acceleration
Beschleunigung
accessible
zugänglich; erreichbar
accidentally
zufällig, aus Versehen
accompany
begleiten
accomplish a task
eine Aufgabe erfüllen
accustomed to
gewöhnt an
achieve
erreichen, leisten
achievement
Leistung; Errungenschaft
acquainted with
vertraut, bekannt mit
acquire experience
Erfahrung erwerben
acumen
Urteilskraft, Scharfsinn
adapt to
anpassen an
adjust
anpassen
admit
zugeben
advance; in ~
im voraus
advantage
Vorteil
adventurous
abenteuerlustig, abenteuerlich
advertise
annoncieren
advice
Rat
advise
raten
affect
beinflussen, beeinträchtigen
after sales
Kundendienst
aim (to)
Ziel; zielen; streben (nach)
all-male; an ~ jury
eine rein männliche Jury
allocate punishments
Strafen austeilen
allusion
Anspielung
ambitious
ehrgeizig
amount
Betrag
amount to
sich belaufen auf
anchor
verankern; Anker
anniversary
Jubiläum, Geburtstag
announce the theme
das Thema ankündigen
annual
jährlich
ant
Ameise
anxious
ängstlich; gespannt
anxious to do
begierig sein, etwas zu tun
apart from
abgesehen von
apology
Entschuldigung
appeal to
appellieren an
appeal to emotions
die Gefühle ansprechen
appearance
Erscheinung; Äußeres; Auftritt
apply
sich bewerben; anwenden
apply pressure
hier: Bremskraft übertragen
apply for a position
sich für einen Posten bewerben
appoint someone
jemanden ernennen
appointment
Termin, Verabredung
appreciate something
dankbar sein für, etwas zu schätzen wissen
appreciation
Anerkennung; Dankbarkeit

appreciative
dankbar; anerkennend
approach
Methode; Ansatz
appropriate
passend, angemessen
appropriation
Aneignung; Verwendung
approximately
ungefähr, annähernd
apt
passend, angemessen
argue
streiten; argumentieren
arouse interest
Interesse wecken
arrow
Pfeil
ashamed; be ~ of
sich schämen für
asset
Vorteil; Aktivposten
assurance
Gewißheit, Versicherung
attend
besuchen; anwesend sein
attention
Aufmerksamkeit
attitude
Einstellung, Haltung
average
Durchschnitt; durchschnittlich
avoid
vermeiden
award
Preis, Auszeichnung
award a prize
einen Preis verleihen
awkward; an ~ silence
eine peinliche Stille

B

bald
kahlköpfig
barefoot
barfuß
bear with someone
Geduld haben mit jemandem
beat about the bush
um den heißen Brei reden
behalf; on ~ of
im Namen von
behaviour
Benehmen, Verhalten
beneficial
vorteilhaft
benefit
Nutzen, Vorteil; profitieren
benefit; give someone the ~ of ...
jemanden in den Genuß von ... kommen lassen
bill
Rechnung
blame; take the ~
die Schuld auf sich nehmen
blunder
Fehler, Schnitzer
body language
Körpersprache
body of a speech
Hauptteil einer Rede
bond
Bindung
bonus scheme
Prämiensystem
bore someone
jemanden langweilen
both
beide
bottom
Boden, Grund
bound; be ~ to be
sein müssen
boundary
Grenze
bow
sich verbeugen
brain
Gehirn
braking pressure
Bremskraft
breach
Bresche
breadth
Breite
break down
zusammenbrechen
break something down
auflisten, gruppieren, ordnen
breakthrough; a technical ~
ein technischer Durchbruch

brick
Ziegelstein
bride
Braut
brief
kurz
brief someone
jemanden informieren
brim, keep the cup brimming
immer etwas im Becher haben; immer guter Laune sein
broken down by age
aufgeschlüsselt nach Alter; altersschwach
budget; keeping within the ~
das Budget nicht überschreiten
bull; take the ~ by the horns
den Stier bei den Hörnern packen
bully someone
jemanden schikanieren
bumper bar
Stoßstange
bustle with
wimmeln von

C

cancel
absagen, stornieren
capacity; in one's ~ as
in seiner Eigenschaft als
caretaker
Hausmeister
carry forward a meeting
eine Besprechung vorverlegen
cart-horse
Kutschengaul
case
Kasten, Kiste; Fall; Prozeß
cast one's eyes over something
etwas betrachten
cast someone in a cell
jemanden in eine Gefängniszelle sperren
cause and effect
Ursache und Wirkung
celebrate
feiern
celebration
Feier
century
Jahrhundert
chair; take the ~
den Vorsitz führen
chairperson
Vorsitzende(r)
challenge
Herausforderung
check out
überprüfen
cherry tree
Kirschbaum
chin up!
Kopf hoch!
choice
Wahl
circumstance
Umstand
civil servant
Beamter
claim
behaupten
clap
klatschen
clarify
erläutern, klären
clergyman
Geistlicher
climax
Höhepunkt
close; bring to a close
zum Abschluß bringen; zu Ende führen
closing; a ~ word
ein abschließendes Wort
cog, a ~ in the machine
ein Rädchen im Getriebe
commit oneself
sich festlegen
committed; be ~
engagiert sein
common good; work for the ~ ~
für das gemeinsame Wohl arbeiten
comparatively
vergleichsweise
comparison
Vergleich
compete with
konkurrieren mit
competition
Wettbewerb

complaint
Beschwerde, Reklamation
complement each other
sich gegenseitig ergänzen
complete a project
ein Projekt zu Ende führen
compliment entry
einleitendes Kompliment
concerned at
besorgt; betroffen über
conclusion
Schluß; Abschluß
confidence; have ~ in ...
Vertrauen haben in ...
conquer terrestrial opponents
Gegner zu Lande erobern
consider
betrachten; in Erwägung ziehen
considerable
beachtlich
consideration; treat with ~
rücksichtsvoll behandeln
consist of
bestehen aus
contagious
ansteckend
content (Betonung auf 2. Silbe)
Zufriedenheit; zufrieden
content (Betonung auf 1. Silbe)
Inhalt
contribute
beitragen
contribution
Beitrag
convention
Versammlung; Kongreß
convey
mitteilen; vermitteln
convince
überzeugen
cope with a situation
einer Situation gewachsen sein
copy writers
Werbetexter
cord
Schnur, Strick
couple with
verbinden mit
counsel
Rat
count on
zählen auf
credibility
Glaubwürdigkeit
credible
glaubwürdig
crucial; a ~ moment
eine entscheidender Augenblick
cruising speed
Reisegeschwindigkeit
cuff; speak off the ~
aus dem Stegreif sprechen
customer
Kunde

D

Day of Judgement
Jüngstes Gericht
deaf
taub
deal someone a blow
jemandem einen Schlag versetzen
dear
lieb, teuer
decade
Jahrzehnt
decision
Entscheidung
decisively, act ~
entschlossen handeln
decorate
schmücken; tapezieren
dedicated
engagiert
dedication
Pflichtbewußtsein; Engagement
deliberately
absichtlich
delicate; a ~ task
eine heikle Aufgabe
delight
Entzücken, Freude
delighted
entzückt
deliver a speech
eine Rede halten
delivery problem
Lieferproblem

departure
Weggang, Abreise
depend on
abhängen von
depth
Tiefe
describe
beschreiben
description
Beschreibung
deserve praise
Lob verdienen
despair
Verzweiflung
destiny
Schicksal
destructive
zerstörerisch
detect mistakes
Fehler entdecken
determination
Entschlossenheit
device
Gerät, Vorrichtung
devoid; be ~ of
etwas entbehren
devotion
Hingabe
digest
verdauen
dine and wine
dinieren, vornehm speisen
disappear
verschwinden
disappointed
enttäuscht
disbelief
Unglaube
discovery
Entdeckung
disk
Scheibe
dismissal
Entlassung
dissatisfied
unzufrieden
distinguished;
a ~ audience
ein vornehmes Publikum
distribution
Vertrieb; Verteilung
divisional leader
Bereichsleiter
do one's bit
seine Aufgaben machen
donate
spenden
donation
Spende
Don't get me wrong.
Verstehen Sie mich nicht falsch.
door latch
Türangel
down payment
Anzahlung
downtown
Stadtzentrum
doze off
einnicken
draft
Entwurf; entwerfen, aufsetzen
draw lots
losen
drug dealers
Drogenhändler

E

earn money
Geld verdienen
earn one's living
seinen Lebensunterhalt verdienen
edit
überarbeiten
efficiency
Leistungsfähigkeit
ejector seat
Schleudersitz
elapse; time has ~
Zeit ist verstrichen
eloquent
beredsam
embarrassed
verlegen, peinlich berührt
embarrassing
peinlich
emit pollution
Umweltgifte ausstoßen
emphasis
Betonung, Hervorhebung
emphasise
betonen
enhanced quality
verbesserte Qualität
enjoy oneself
sich amüsieren
enlarge
vergrößern

enterprise
Unternehmen; Unternehmung
entrepreneur
Unternehmer
entry
Eingang; Anfang
environment
Umgebung; Umwelt
environmental publicity
Veröffentlichungen zum Umweltschutz
estimate
abschätzen
even if
selbst wenn
event
Ereignis
Every cloud has a silver lining.
Nach Regen kommt auch wieder Sonnenschein.
evidence
Beweis; Zeugnis; Aussage
evil
Übel; böse
evil-doers
Übeltäter
executive
leitender Angestellter
exhaust
Abgase
expand
erweitern, ausdehnen
expansion
Ausdehnung, Erweiterung
expense
Ausgaben
experience
Erfahrung
extend
erweitern, ausdehnen
extend a hearty thankyou
ein herzliches Dankeschön sagen

F

fade out
hier: in den Hintergrund treten, sich zurückziehen
fall flat (joke)
nicht ankommen (Witz)
favour; do a ~
einen Gefallen tun
features
Eigenschaften (eines Produkts)
fee
Honorar
feedback
Rückmeldung
fellow sufferer
Leidensgenosse
figure
Zahl
figures of speech
Stilfiguren
flatter
schmeicheln
flattery
Schmeichelei
fly
Fliege; fliegen
floor, take the ~
das Wort ergreifen
flop
Reinfall; Mißerfolg
foam
Schaum
fond; grow ~ of
liebgewinnen
fool
Narr, Dummkopf
fool someone
jemanden zum Narren halten
foolproof
idiotensicher
foreign
fremd, ausländisch
foreigner
Ausländer, Fremder
forge
schmieden
forgiveness
Vergebung
forthcoming; a ~ marriage
eine bevorstehende Heirat
foundation stone
Grundstein
founder
Gründer(in)
four-wheel drive
Vierradantrieb
framework
Rahmen
fulfilment
Erfüllung

funeral
Begräbnis
furious
wütend
furniture
Möbel

G

gap
Lücke
gathering
Zusammenkunft, Versammlung
gear transmission
Getriebe
gear-wheel
Zahnrad
generous
großzügig
genuinely
ehrlich, aufrichtig
gesture
Geste, Bewegung
get-together
Zusammenkunft
gift
Geschenk
gist
Kern der Sache
gnashing of teeth
Zähneknirschen
go public
an die Öffentlichkeit treten
goal
Ziel
goodwill
Kulanz; Kooperationsbereitschaft
grab the bull by the horns
den Stier bei den Hörnern packen
grass roots
Fußvolk
grateful
dankbar
gratitude
Dankbarkeit
greenbacks
Blaumänner
grip; lose one's ~
seinen Halt verlieren
groom, bridegroom
Bräutigam
gruelling; a ~ examination
ein hartes Examen
grunt
grunzen
guidance
Führung
guide the attention
die Aufmerksamkeit lenken

H

habit
Gewohnheit
handout
Tischvorlage
happiness
Freude, Glück
have what it takes to …
das Zeug haben zu …
head of department
Abteilungsleiter
health
Gesundheit
heart; learn by ~
auswendig lernen
height
Höhe
helm; take the ~
das Ruder übernehmen
hesitation
Zögern
Hide and Seek
Versteckspiel
highlight
hervorheben
hint
Hinweis
hit the target
ins Schwarze treffen
hold water
hieb und stichfest, stichhaltig
honesty
Ehrlichkeit
honorary guest
Ehrengast
honour
Ehre
honourable
ehrenwert
Honourable Spectators
verehrte Zuschauer
honoured; be ~
sich geehrt fühlen
host
Gastgeber; Moderator

hot
heiß; scharf
HQ
Zentrale
hum; the ~ of the market
das geschäftige Summen des Markts
humanity
Menschlichkeit; Menschheit

I

ignorant
unwissend
impression
Eindruck
in spite of
trotz
inappropriate
unangemessen
inaugural address
Rede zur Amtseinführung
inauguration
Einweihung; Amtseinführung
incline to
neigen zu
include
umfassen; einschließen
increase
zunehmen, steigen
increase the turnover
den Umsatz steigern
indicate
an-/aufzeigen
indispensable
unentbehrlich
innings, my ~ has come to an end
(Kricket) meine Zeit geht zu Ende
instead
anstatt
instruct
anweisen
instrumental
hilfreich
insurance
Versicherung
intend
beabsichtigen
intent
Absicht, Anliegen
interruption
Unterbrechung
intruder
Eindringling
inventor
Erfinder
involve; the costs involved
die damit verbundenen Kosten
involved; all ~
alle Beteiligten
involved; be closely ~ in ...
eng mit ... befaßt, beteiligt sein
issue
Thema; Problem; Frage

J

join a company
in eine Firma eintreten
joking apart
Spaß beiseite
joy
Freude
judgement
Urteil; Urteilskraft

K

keep within the budget
das Budget nicht überschreiten
keystone
Grundstein

L

labour dispute
Arbeitskampf
lasting; a ~ part
ein bleibender Teil
laudable
lobenswert
launch a product
ein Produkt einführen
lawn
Rasen
lay off employees
Angestellte entlassen
laziness
Faulheit
length
Länge
less tax
weniger Steuern

let out all the stops
Dampf machen, Vollgas geben
library
Bibliothek
lie
Lüge; lügen
link
Verbindung
link in a chain
Glied in einer Kette
lose sight of ...
aus den Augen verlieren
lose, lost, lost
verlieren
loyalty
Treue

M

make liberal use of
großzügigen Gebrauch machen von
male voice
männliche Stimme
marble
Marmor
masterpiece
Meisterwerk
match
übereinstimmen
meditative mood
nachdenkliche Stimmung
memorable
denk-, merkwürdig
memory
Gedächtnis
mention
erwähnen
merit an award
eine Auszeichnung verdienen
misfortune
Unglück
mission statement
Verkündung des Unternehmensziels
mortar
Mörtel
musical chairs; play ~ ~
Reise nach Jerusalem spielen
mutual co-operation
wechselseitige Zusammenarbeit
mutual(ly)
gegenseitig, wechselseitig

N

nap
Nickerchen
native speaker
Muttersprachler
neat
ordentlich
needs
Bedürfnisse
negotiate
verhandeln
nevertheless
nichtsdestoweniger
niceties
Nettigkeit; Artigkeit
nostalgic
wehmütig
nuisance
Ärgernis

O

obituary
Todesanzeige
objection
Einwand
objective
Ziel
observer
Beobachter
obvious(ly)
offensichtlich
occasion
Anlaß
on behalf of
im Namen von
one-syllable word
einsilbiges Wort
opportunity
(günstige) Gelegenheit
opposite
Gegenteil
opt for
sich entscheiden für
Order!
Ruhe!
ornament
Schmuck, Zierat
outline
Gliederung
overcome one's fear
seine Furcht überwinden

oversight
Versehen
overwhelmed
überwältigt
owe something to someone
jemandem etwas schulden, verdanken
own; be on one's ~
auf sich allein gestellt sein

P

pale
blaß
pancake
Pfannkuchen
panel of judges
Jury
parcel up
verpacken
partake of a dinner
sich an einem Diner erfreuen/gütlich tun
participant
Teilnehmer
participate in
teilnehmen an, Anteil haben an
particular(ly)
besonders
parting
Abschied
pass away
sterben, verscheiden
pavilion
hier (Kricket): Zelt mit Erfrischungen für die Spieler
pay tribute to
jemandem Tribut, Respekt zollen
pep talk
Motivations-, Aufmunterungsrede
performance
Leistung
perhaps
vielleicht
persuade
überreden
persuasion
Überredung; Überzeugung
petrol
Benzin
pipeline; in the ~
in Bearbeitung, auf dem Weg sein
plain
schlicht
plunge
Sprung (ins Wasser)
poet
Dichter
poetic licence
dichterische Freiheit
pope
Papst
possibility
Möglichkeit
potential clients
potentielle Kunden
pottery
Töpferei
poverty
Armut
practice; it is normal ~
es ist üblich
praise
Lob; loben
praise; deserve ~
Lob verdienen
prayer
Gebet
predecessor
Vorgänger
prefer
vorziehen, lieber tun
pretend
vorgeben, so tun als ob
prevent
verhindern
previous
vorherig, früher
previous speaker
Vorredner
primarily
in erster Linie, primär
prioritise
Prioritäten setzen
prize
Preis, Auszeichnung
processes
Geschäftsabläufe
profound thoughts
tiefschürfende Gedanken
promote
befördern; fördern
propose the health of someone
auf jemandes Wohl trinken

prospective; a ~ candidate
ein angehender Kandidat
prosperity
Wohlergehen, Wohlstand
protector
Beschützer
proud
stolz
provide
zur Verfügung stellen
provide someone with something
jemanden mit etwas versorgen
provision for taxes
Steuerrücklage
provoke
provozieren
puberty
Pubertät
pull together
am gleichen Strang ziehen
purchase
einkaufen; Kauf; Einkauf
purchasing department
Einkaufsabteilung
purpose
Ziel, Zweck
put up with something
etwas aushalten, ertragen

Q

quieten down
sich beruhigen
quit
weggehen, verlassen, aufgeben
quotation; quote
Zitat

R

rack
Kleiderstange; Zahnstange
raise arguments against …
Argumente gegen … vorbringen
raise money
Geld aufbringen
raise one's glass
sein Glas erheben
raisin
Rosine
range
Reihe; Produktpalette
rapids
Stromschnellen
rear to go
ungeduldig warten auf
recipient
Empfänger
recognise
wieder-/anerkennen
recommend
empfehlen
reconnaissance
Erkundung
record
bekunden; aufnehmen (Tonband)
red tape
Bürokratie; Papierkram
reduce
verringern, (ver)kürzen
refer to (the fact that …)
verweisen auf, sich beziehen auf
refer to the handouts
auf die Tischvorlagen verweisen
reference
Verweis, Hinweis, Bezug
reflect
widerspiegeln
reflect a person's value
den Wert einer Person widerspiegeln
refrain from doing something
etwas unterlassen
refuse
sich weigern, ablehnen; Abfall
register
Stilebene
regret
bedauern; Reue
rehearse the speech
die Rede proben
relationship
Beziehung
relaxed
entspannt
reliability
Zuverlässigkeit

relief
Erleichterung
remark
bemerken; Bemerkung
remove
entfernen
replace
ersetzen
reply
Antwort
reputation
Ruf, Ansehen
request someone's help
um jemandes Hilfe bitten
requested; be ~ to do something
gebeten werden, etwas zu tun
require
erfordern; verlangen, erbitten
require considerable skill
erhebliches Geschick erfordern
requirement
Bedarf; Bedürfnis; (An-)Forderung; Voraussetzung
resignation
Rücktritt
resistance
Widerstand, Ablehnung
response
Erwiderung; Reaktion
responsible
verantwortlich, verantwortungsvoll
retire
in den Ruhestand treten; sich zurückziehen
retirement
Ruhestand, Pensionierung
retort
Erwiderung; erwidern
return
Gewinn, Ertrag; Rückkehr
reveal
verraten, preisgeben, enthüllen
reward
Belohnung
ribbon cutting
Durchschneiden des Bandes
ridicule
verspotten
roar
brüllen
root
Wurzel
rowdy
rüpelhaft
rude(ly)
grob, unhöflich
rule
Regel
rumour
Gerücht

S

sales force
Verkaufsteam
scrape
kratzen
selective
wählerisch
selfishness
Egoismus
sense
empfinden, fühlen; Sinn
sequence
Folge
serious
ernst
sermon
Predigt
service; old in ~
alt an Dienstjahren
set priorities
Prioritäten setzen
set the tone
den Ton angeben
setback
Rückschlag
settle in
sich eingewöhnen
shake
schütteln
share
Anteil; teilen
shareholder
Aktionär
shift
Schicht
shoe-size
Schuhgröße
shot; take a ~ at
bei etwas zugreifen
show off
angeben

showroom
Ausstellungsraum
shrewd foresight
scharfer Weitblick
shut up
den Mund halten
simile
bildhafter Vergleich
sincere
aufrichtig; ehrlich
sincerity
Aufrichtigkeit
sing someone's praises
Lobeshymnen auf jemanden singen
skirt
Rock
sleepwalk
schlafwandeln
sleeve; have something up one's ~
etwas in der Hinterhand haben
slide
Diapositiv
slip
Versprecher; Fehler
slope
Hang (eines Berges)
snake skin
Schlangenhaut
snappy quotations
pfiffige Zitate
sober
nüchtern
soften a statement
eine Äußerung abschwächen, mildern
solemn moment
feierlicher Moment
solution
Lösung
solve a problem
ein Problem lösen
source of enjoyment
Quelle der Freude
spade; call a ~ a ~
die Dinge beim Namen nennen
speak fluently
flüssig sprechen
specs, specifications
technische Eigenschaften; Lastenheft
speechmaker
Redner
spite; in ~ of
trotz
spread
verteilen
squarely; look the problem ~ in the eye
dem Problem gerade ins Auge schauen
staff
Belegschaft
stage fright
Lampenfieber
stake
Anteil; Pfahl
stapler
Hefter; Tucker
steal the limelight from someone
jemandem die Schau stehlen
steer round problems
Problemen ausweichen
still
jedoch; noch
stimulate
anregen
stomach ache
Bauchschmerzen
straight; come ~ to the point
sofort zur Sache kommen
street; be up somebody's ~
in jemandes Fach schlagen
strenuously
emsig, tatkräftig, energisch
stress
betonen; Betonung; Streß
stride forwards into the future
in die Zukunft schreiten
strike, struck, struck
auffallen; schlagen
struggle through
sich durchkämpfen
substitute
Ersatz
success
Erfolg
suffer from
leiden an/unter
suggest
vorschlagen, anregen; andeuten

suggestions
Vorschläge, Anregungen
suit
Anzug
suit the occasion
zum Anlaß passen
suitable quotation
passendes Zitat
summarise
zusammenfassen
supplier
Lieferant
support
Unterstützung; unterstützen
supposed; be ~ to do something
etwas tun sollen
surprise
Überraschung
survive
überleben
suspense
Spannung
sustain a loss
einen Verlust erleiden

T

take; have what it takes to ...
das Zeug haben zu ...
take place
stattfinden
talk shop
fachsimpeln
target
Ziel
target; be on ~
genau treffen
targeted at all markets
für alle Märkte bestimmt
temper
Laune
testimonial
Referenz, Empfehlung, Empfehlungsschreiben
testimony
Zeugnis, Referenz
the incoming president
der künftige Präsident
thoroughbred
Rassepferd, Araber
thread
Faden
tin-opener
Büchsenöffner
tiring
ermüdend
toastmaster
Moderator, Zeremonienmeister
token of esteem
Zeichen der Wertschätzung
top of the range
Flaggschiff (der Produktpalette)
topic
Thema
trade union
Gewerkschaft
trainee
Auszubildender
transfer to HQ
in die Zentrale wechseln
transferred to Headquarters
versetzt zur Zentrale
trapped
gefangen, eingeklemmt
treat as ...
behandeln als ...
tremendous
gewaltig
tremendous ovation
enormer Applaus
trophy
Trophäe
trowel
Kelle
trust
trauen, vertrauen
turn someone away
jemanden abweisen
turnover
Umsatz
twice
zweimal
twilight
Dämmerung; Zwielicht

U

unconcerned
ungerührt
undisturbed
störungsfrei, reibungslos
unfounded
unbegründet
uninhibited applause
rückhaltloser Applaus
union representative
Gewerkschaftsvertreter

unit
Abteilung
unpleasant
unerfreulich, unangenehm
unsatisfactory
unbefriedigend
untrue
unwahr
upgrade
verbessern

V

vacancy
freie Stelle
vacuum cleaner
Staubsauger
valuable
wertvoll
value
Wert
vary
wechseln, variieren
ventilated
belüftet
verge; be on the ~ of doing something
im Begriff sein, etwas zu tun
verify
nachprüfen
vital
wichtig, wesentlich
voice
Stimme

W

wallet
Brieftasche
wedding
Hochzeit
weight
Gewicht
well-kept
gepflegt
wheel
Rad
whip up support for someone
um Unterstützung für … werben
wild cat strike
wilder Streik
work to rule
Dienst nach Vorschrift
worthwhile
der Mühe wert

Y

yet
jedoch

Z

zero
Null
zip
Reißverschluß